painting pictures with words makes you feel at home, whether visiting eateries, bookshops, jewelry stores, or the Selkirk Arms. It's with a sense of sadness that you board the plane to fly home. I long to visit Galloway, but reading this delightful description of the land and the people is the next best thing!"

—NANCY MACCLELLAN SEARS, treasurer, Clan MacLellan

"A bonny blend of Liz's lyrical fiction and tantalizing Scotland facts told in an intimate style. Not only do we explore a beautiful country, but we also discover treasures about Liz Curtis Higgs. With her wit and stories, Liz charms residents and booksellers, just as she charms readers. After reading this book, I'd put my luggage in the right-hand-driving-car boot next to Liz's anytime. In fact, I feel as if I have."

—JANE KIRKPATRICK, author of *All Together in One Place*

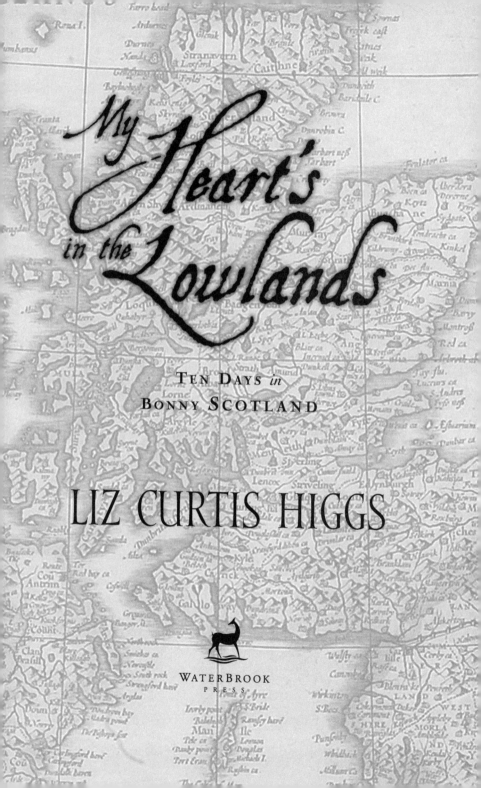

My Heart's in the Lowlands

Ten Days in Bonny Scotland

LIZ CURTIS HIGGS

WaterBrook
PRESS

MY HEART'S IN THE LOWLANDS
PUBLISHED BY WATERBROOK PRESS
12265 Oracle Boulevard, Suite 200
Colorado Springs, Colorado 80921
A division of Random House Inc.

ISBN 978-1-4000-7297-2

Library of Congress Cataloguing-in-Publication Data
Higgs, Liz Curtis.
   My heart's in the lowlands : ten days in bonny Scotland / Liz Curtis Higgs. — 1st ed.
      p. cm.
   Includes bibliographical references.
   ISBN-13: 978-1-4000-7297-2
   1. Galloway (Scotland)—Description and travel. 2. Galloway (Scotland)—Social life and
customs. 3. Lowlands (Scotland)—Description and travel. 4. Lowlands (Scotland)—Social
life and customs. I. Title.
   DA880.G1H54 2007
   941.4'7086092—dc22
   [B]
                                        2006032097

Printed in the United States of America
2007—First Edition

10 9 8 7 6 5 4 3 2 1

MEET LIZ

Liz Curtis Higgs fell in love with Scotland more than a decade ago when she began researching the Lowlands for a series of historical novels. Her luminous and vivid storytelling has transported countless readers to her adopted homeland through the rich details gathered on her many trips to the region, including her twelve-city "Heart for Scotland" book tour.

A busy conference speaker, Liz has addressed audiences in all fifty states and eight foreign countries. She is the author of twenty-five books, with more than three million copies in print, including her nonfiction bestseller, *Bad Girls of the Bible,* and her Christy Award–winning novel, *Whence Came a Prince.* Liz and her husband, Bill, share their nineteenth-century farmhouse in Kentucky with two teenagers, Matt and Lilly, and too many cats.

CONTENTS

An Invitation 1

First Light 7

Heading South 14

Second Breakfast 22

To Kirk We Go 29

Country and Town 39

Burns Slept Here...and Here 47

Homeward Bound 56

A Sense of Place 60

In a Fog 68

Holy Ground 73

Gilded Arches 80

History Lesson 91

Burgh of Barony 99

Sunlight and Shadow 105

Under the Weather 111

Storming the Bookshop 117

A Misty Afternoon 124

Of Smugglers and Monks 130

New in Town 137

On the High Street 143

Making History 152

Over the Hill 159

Fair Anwoth 165

Castle and Cairn 175

Ferry Thorn 182

Into the Glen 187

She Walks These Hills 193

Auld Kirk, New Kirk 201

Wild and Woolly 209

An Afternoon of Villages 216

Banks o' the Nith 226

Looking North 236

Haste Ye Back 245

A Wee Word 247

Notes 251

Glossary 257

O Scotia!…

For whom my warmest wish

to Heaven is sent!

ROBERT BURNS

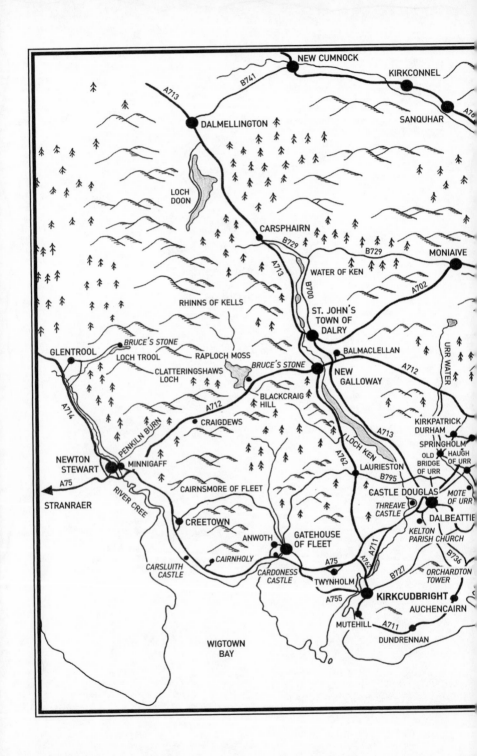

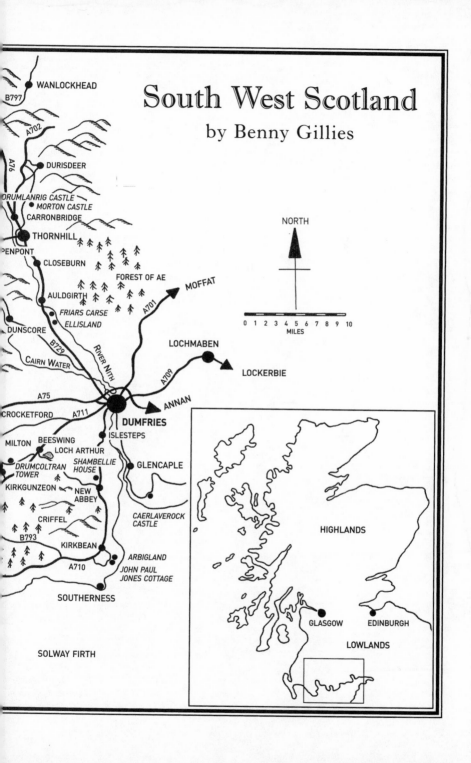

South West Scotland
by Benny Gillies

AN INVITATION

But first, before you see heaven's glory,

May ye get mony a merry story.

ROBERT BURNS

*L*iz, are you off to Scotland *again*?"

I blush to confess it. *Aye.*

At first everyone understood. "Doing research for your novels," they said. Who wouldn't enjoy seeing the land of *Braveheart* and *Rob Roy*?

But when my visits became an annual pilgrimage, when every spare penny and frequent-flier mile was earmarked "Glasgow," when I had to build more bookshelves to hold all my treasured tomes from you-know-where, one fact became abundantly clear: Scotland had captured my heart and was not about to let go.

So…let's *go,* shall we? Just the two of us?

Rather than running breathlessly from one end of the country to the other, we'll take a leisurely turn around South West Scotland, known as Dumfries and Galloway. Many travelers bypass this quiet corner, eager to experience the stark beauty of the Highlands—a sight worth seeing, to be sure. But I consider Galloway the country's best-kept secret: a place where time holds its breath, where ancient ruins dot the countryside in moss-covered splendor, where the natives are friendly and the tourists are few, only because they don't know what they're missing.

So, ten days in bonny Scotland. You'll join me, aye?

May is the best month for a leap across the pond. The sun rises by five and tarries past nine, providing ample time to wander down every footpath that beckons. The air is scented with lilacs. Month-old lambs gambol along the hedgerows, and the rolling hills and glens are covered with the greenest grass you can imagine.

I'm on tiptoe just thinking about it.

Don't worry about the driving; a steering wheel on the right side of the car and traffic on the left side of the road feel perfectly natural to me. Besides, in May we'll have the place to ourselves. Students are still in school, and most tourists wait for summer. English sightseers, however, barrel up the M6 motorway on the weekends, so we'll plan to arrive on a Sunday and depart on a Tuesday. That will give us lots of weekdays to poke about the village shops and explore half a dozen castles and linger over pots of tea and nibble on scones and…

Oh, is it May yet?

GLASGOW BOUND

It's always May, if only in our hearts.

Our Continental flight leaves in an hour, and the passengers in the gate area are growing restless. The novel stuffed in my purse remains untouched, yet my plane ticket has been consulted many times. *Still safely in place. Still a 7:50 p.m. departure.*

Behind us, a Glaswegian woman scolds her teenage sons for wandering off. *"Eejits!"* she fumes. "Are ye daft?"

I duck my head to hide a smile and see you do the same. No matter the dialect, a mother's words are universal.

When the first wave of passengers begins to board, we gather our belongings and follow the herd, trying not to be envious of all that legroom in the business-class cabin. No matter. Business or coach, high road or low road, we'll all be in Scotland afore long.

Truly, that's all that matters.

"WHY SCOTLAND, LIZ?"

I'm asked that question so often I really should have a snappy answer at the ready. "Because it's the loveliest place on earth" is a beginning. "Because I'm fascinated by the country's history" offers some justification. "Because men in kilts make my heart skip a beat" may be true, though it's the skirl of a lone bagpipe that brings a lump to my throat. Crawfords and Walkers, two fine Lowland names, grow in my family tree, but we've yet to find our roots definitively planted in Caledonian soil.

How then to explain my abiding affection for Scotland, a country small enough to fit inside the state of Indiana with room to spare?

Perhaps because when I'm there, I have a sense of rightness, of completion, of belonging.

The verdant, rolling hills remind me of places I've lived—eastern Pennsylvania and central Kentucky in particular—yet the angle of the sun falling across the Lowland moors is uniquely Scottish. That slanted light works a kind of magic on me. The misty air softens my complexion. Sleep comes easily. Contentment seeps into my bones. I bite into a freshly baked oatcake, covered with a generous slice of sharp Galloway cheese, then sip milk-laced tea, hot enough to numb my lips, and I'm within walking distance of heaven.

I've felt this way since May 1996 when I first crossed the English border, driving north from Manchester Airport, and was greeted by a sign shaped like an arched door bearing a regal red lion and a single word in bold letters: SCOTLAND. I parked on the shoulder of the road, hands trembling as I photographed the sign, and then I wept with joy.

Home, home, home.

A good friend of mine feels the same way about Italy, and another adores a certain island in the Caribbean. For me, it will always be Scotland— Galloway in particular. The musical lilt of a Lowland accent never fails to boost my spirits. I'm simply, deliriously *happy* there. I suspect you share my passion for all things Scottish, or you wouldn't be traveling with me now, bound for a distant kingdom.

Bless you for coming, my friend.

Counting the Hours

As we settle into our coach-cabin seats, the screen in front of us displays a map of the eastern half of the United States and the western half of Europe, with a dotted line showing our intended route arching over New England before heading out to sea. We'll cover a daunting number of miles tonight: more than three thousand. Had fictional Jamie McKie, the hero from my Lowlands of Scotland novels, sailed across the Atlantic in the late eighteenth century, the crossing would have taken two months. Hard to fathom we'll cover the same distance in mere hours.

Dinner, such as it is, will come and go soon after takeoff. Might be a good idea to set our watches on Glasgow time—five hours later than New York—if only to remind us it's already 1:00 a.m. where we're headed. Sleep is a must, or we'll spend our first day in a jet-lagged stupor.

I gaze out the window as we taxi from the gate, anticipation thrumming inside me. In little more than six hours we'll begin our descent over the Firth of Clyde and across the hilly moors of west Renfrewshire, a bolt of green velvet undulating beneath our wings. Unless it's a foggy morning, the sun will be shining in our pilot's eyes when the wheels meet the runway with a firm bounce and the flight attendant announces our arrival at Glasgow International Airport.

Sleep? Who am I kidding?

We're flying toward Scotland. We're flying toward dawn.

> The sky was a luminous dark blue with a faint pattern
> of clouds. As Leana watched, the color changed to
> turquoise so gradually she could not discern how or

when it happened. Yet when she looked down for a moment to brush a leaf from her lap, then looked up again, the sky was lighter. And fading to gray.

Leana heard footsteps. Then Jamie's voice. "'Tis a beautiful sight first thing in the morning."

Whence Came a Prince

FIRST LIGHT

Sleep'st thou, or wak'st thou, fairest creature?
Rosy morn now lifts his eye.

ROBERT BURNS

J awaken to find my cheek pressed against the closed window
shade, the flimsy airline pillow having disappeared over the far
side of my armrest. Inching the vinyl shade upward, blinking as light
streams in, I remind myself it only *feels* as if we've lost a whole day.

Scotland on Sunday. That's the newspaper we'll snag once we're inside
the terminal.

Peering down through the thick cloud cover, we're rewarded with our
first, fleeting glimpse of land: two coastal islands, Great Cumbrae and
Little Cumbrae, set amid a shimmering sea. Then the mainland appears,
dotted with countless lochs, like puddles of silver surrounded by green.

When the wheels are lowered with a mechanical whir and the ground rises closer, my heart is about to burst. *Home, indeed.*

Moments later we're taxiing toward the gate. No question where we've landed: all the Jetways are emblazoned with the Royal Bank of Scotland logo. Inside the airport a blue and white sign at the head of the staircase proclaims, "Welcome to Scotland: The best small country in the world." Low-ceilinged corridors boast colorful images of tartans, bagpipes, and Highland dancers. The occasional *HM* for "Her Majesty" reminds us that Scotland is part of the United Kingdom, though it's clearly a country unto itself.

We make a quick stop in the *loo*—brightly lit and fresh smelling, with long, skinny stalls and round-seated toilets—then join the throng heading for Passport Control.

Around us, sleep-deprived voices sound gravelly. Shoulders are slumped, gaits stiff. When we hand over the simple immigration forms, filled out on the plane, we're greeted with a cheery hello and a stamp of approval on our passports—a smudgy, black square giving us leave to enter the country for six months. Oh, to have the resources to manage *that.* Still, our ten days will do nicely.

Now it's time to start praying, not because it's Sunday, but because we're standing at Baggage Reclaim. Anxious faces scrutinize the many-bags-look-alike parade as it passes by. One memorable January morning I landed in Glasgow, but my luggage landed in Edinburgh. Visions of wearing the same clothes for a week flickered through my head until I arrived at my bed-and-breakfast later that afternoon and found a good-natured taxi driver delivering my errant suitcases.

When you spot your luggage, your relief is understandable. My own black bag is not far behind; the polka-dotted ribbon on the handle makes it easy to spot. It's heavier than I remembered; too many books in a suitcase will do that. I seldom break my five-outfits-a-trip rule, but I always feel compelled to add just one more book.

Highways and Byways in Galloway and Carrick is a favorite. Written by Rev. Charles Hill Dick in 1916, the small clothbound book fits neatly in my purse. Never mind that the cover is stained with mildew; this wee green volume is a literary jewel, filled with sketches and picturesque phrases like "a distant jumble of whitewashed cottages standing against the shining Firth."[1] Rev. Dick, who toured Galloway on a bicycle, describes the land and its people in delightful detail. His style of prose is a throwback to a gentler time and place: "After these extracts from the musty folios of the town council records, it is pleasant to return to the open air and advise the reader about some little journeys in the neighbourhood."[2] Such eloquent wording warms my English-major heart. Though I have no plans to ride a bicycle, highways and byways we shall see, dearie.

OF MAPS AND COINS

Belongings in tow, we head for the newsagent and stock up on newspapers, breath mints, and Ordnance Survey maps. Great Britain is the best-mapped corner of the globe, and these detailed maps are proof. Ever since King George II commissioned a military survey of the Highlands in 1747 following the Jacobite Rising, mapping the countryside has been a British specialty. Ordnance Survey, or O.S., maps are a road warrior's dream. Motorways and railways, landmarks and properties, waterways

and woods are all carefully marked. We can't get lost—at least not perma-
nently—if we have a few of these in our glove box. I've brought Travelmaster Map 4, *Southern Scotland,* to get us started. We'll need Landranger
Maps 77, 78, 83, and 84 to ramble around Dumfries and Galloway.
About seven pounds sterling each and worth every penny.

Which reminds me: you've brought some British currency, aye?
Obtained from your local bank? Most travelers wait until they arrive and
then find an ATM for a better exchange rate. My fear? I'll forget my card
(which I never use at home) or forget my password (ditto) or get here and
discover the magnetic strip has lost its zip, or I'll drive high and low looking for ATMs, uncommon in the wilds of rural Galloway. So I come prepared, cash in hand.

The multicolored fives, tens, twenties, and fifties are each a different
size, which makes life interesting in your wallet. But it's the coins that
intrigue me. Pounds—also called *quid*—are round and doubly thick, a
pleasing weight in your hand. Fifty-pence coins are thin, silver, and hep-
tagonal, as are the smaller twenty pence. The big, round ten pence over-
states its meager value, the five pence looks like our dime, and the copper
twopence—or *tuppence*—is fun to say, though you're more likely to hear
"two p."

"Are ye from Canada, then?" our friendly cashier inquires.

We'll be asked that again before our trip ends, though more often
folks will hear one word from our lips and ask, "Which part of the States
are you from?" We are *fremmit*—strange, foreign. No use pretending we
blend in, though we can try.

With our collection of maps and luggage in hand, we move toward the

Nothing to Declare exit and share a giddy smile. Beyond the revolving door the Lowlands await.

Outside at Last

The moment we reach the curb, a painted warning shouts from the pavement, "LOOK RIGHT." Indeed, hadn't we just gazed to the left out of habit? We yank each other back as a tour bus charges past, barely slowing down. That's one way to see Scotland but not the method I'd choose. Like Rev. Dick on his bicycle, we'll explore the roads less traveled, the ones no lumbering motor coach would dare attempt. In our European-sized Ford or Volvo or whatever Hertz has for us this morning, we'll put our O.S. maps through their paces, following the yellow lines indicating roads less than four meters wide. Ooh, baby. My kind of byway.

As we roll our luggage past the parking garage, a light breeze ripples the grass, and fluffy white clouds spread across the sky like vanilla icing. The Hertz counter amounts to a freestanding coat closet at the edge of the parking lot—make that *car park*—with a customer-service area big enough for two people, if we deposit our bags outside the door. Behind the counter stands a square-faced woman of middling years in a gray sweater with gold buttons and a Hertz-issued gray and gold scarf. Though we can't see her feet, I'll wager she's wearing a pair of sturdy, thick-soled shoes. She eyes us closely, as if assessing our driving skills. "Ye'll be wantin' to hire a vehicle?"

That threw me on my first visit. *Hire?* As in paying a driver to take me around? "No," I patiently explained, "I'll be driving the car myself."

Now I understand the lingo. "Yes, a compact car, please. Automatic." Driving on the left side of the road is one thing; shifting with my left hand is quite another. Papers signed and keys in hand, we're soon loading our bags into the trunk—well, *boot*—of our hired car. The diminutive size will be a blessing when we navigate village streets.

Odd, isn't it, to climb into the passenger seat from the left? I fear you have the more difficult task on this trip: sitting where the steering wheel should be, with nothing but a concealed airbag in front of you. If you can resist the urge to glance in the mirrors, all of which are pointing in my direction, you should be fine.

And Away We Go

Finding our way out of the airport is the first hurdle. No need to unfold our maps just now; letters and numbers are sufficient: M8, M77, A77, A76. I repeat the route under my breath like a prayer so I'm ready when the first sign appears. *M8…M8…* Notice anything missing? Right you are: no "east" or "west." The signs list only the next city: "M8 Glasgow" or "M8 Greenock." Woe to the driver who doesn't know her geography! On one of my early solo trips via Manchester, I ended up in Wales instead of Scotland. Now when I ask for directions, I jot down letters, numbers, *and* cities.

Once we shoot past the modern industrial fringe around the airport, Scotland will not disappoint. We'll see green and more green, with hills rising in the distance. A bit like Oregon, except for the traffic circles. And people driving on the left. And long, narrow license plates in bright yellow with black lettering.

Though we're headed toward Glasgow, we'll merely wave at her one million citizens in passing. I'm a small-town girl at heart and am eager to introduce you to a particular county in Galloway. The long name is Kirkcudbrightshire, but "the Stewartry" is far easier to say. That's the eastern half of old Galloway; "the Shire," or Wigtownshire, is the western half. It, too, boasts fascinating historic sites—the Torhouse Stone Circle and Saint Ninian's Chapel among them. Yet I confess an inordinate fondness for the land that stretches from the River Cree to the River Nith, from the shores of Loch Doon to the Solway Firth.

Hang on to your seat belt as we approach our first traffic circle and prepare to merge onto the motorway. *M8 Glasgow…M8 Glasgow…*

HEADING SOUTH

Adown winding Nith I did wander
To mark the sweet flowers as they spring.

ROBERT BURNS

Today's weather is quintessentially Scottish: mild yet breezy, with a mix of clouds and sun, gray skies and blue patches. In May, temperatures seldom climb above sixty degrees Fahrenheit, or about fifteen degrees Celsius. Such is the measure of things in the U.K., which became clear the first time I heard a BBC weatherman predict a "balmy twenty-five degrees."

Perhaps a dozen days a year the winds are calm. Otherwise, a capricious breeze can be counted on to undo your hairdo. Not that I have one, mind you. And not that it matters when springtime beckons.

The skies were clear but not bright, as if a thin layer of muslin were stretched above Galloway. Anything might happen on such a day. Brilliant sunshine could appear by noon, only to disappear behind heavy clouds come three o' the clock, followed by a downpour at supper.

Whence Came a Prince

You can see why I love arriving on a Sunday. The traffic is far less challenging, with fewer trucks—*lorries* here—rumbling past at breakneck speed, especially now that we're on the M77, a *dual carriageway* with a grassy median. We smile at the cautionary sign "East Renfrewshire Welcomes Careful Drivers" as we pass herds of grazing cattle congregated on great, lumpy hills. Resisting exits that promise to lead to the A77, we stay our course until the motorway turns into the A77 on its own, taking us through Ayrshire scenes of quiet beauty beneath a canopy of low clouds.

Thirty minutes into our journey, I'm grateful when a traffic circle allows us to skirt busy Kilmarnock without mishap. A fine town full of history, but the last time I traveled there, bound for a book signing, I had 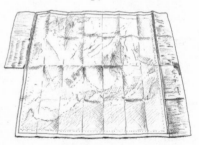 to ring up the bookshop twice for directions, so confusing were the posted signs. Finally they suggested I park at the nearest curb and wait while they sent a kind man in an *estate car*—we'd call it a station wagon—to guide me through the winding streets of Kilmarnock.

"A good number o' folk have come," he told me, escorting me up the stair to John Ritchie's bookshop. Having endured my share of sparsely attended book signings, I prepared myself for the "good number" to be no more than a half dozen. Imagine my astonishment when I discovered more than *three* dozen women nibbling on sandwich triangles and waiting for their American novelist to appear.

Surely it was the sandwiches that drew them. Or the buttery rich shortbread. Or an exceptionally quiet Thursday. Or perhaps it was the giant teakettle—truly the biggest I've ever seen, like those old tin coffee-pots lurking in church basements, except this pot had a long, graceful spout and brewed gallons upon gallons of tea. Whatever coerced those dear women out of their homes on a windy October afternoon, I was bowled over by their warm welcome. Bundled up in their woolen *jumpers*—pullover sweaters—surrounded by brightly colored shelves of books, they graciously listened as I shared the story of how I'd come to write a series of historical novels set in their homeland. If they found my fascination with Scotland over the top, they didn't say so, though they did smile a great deal.

Despite one travel guide's depiction of "the grimly workaday town of Kilmarnock,"[1] I found the place charming. After all, Robert Burns was first published here; *Poems Chiefly in the Scottish Dialect* was printed by John Wilson in Kilmarnock in July 1786. A mere six hundred copies came off the press and sold out just weeks later, putting twenty pounds in the author's pocket. News of his talent quickly traveled to Edinburgh. When Wilson was unwilling to print additional copies of *Poems* unless the paper was paid for in advance, Burns set off on a borrowed pony for Scotland's capital, where he won the hearts of the literati with his rustic poetry and so secured his place as Scotland's bard.

By the way, Burns's lilting song "My Heart's in the Highlands" belies the truth: Burns was a Lowlander, born in Ayrshire and buried in Dumfriesshire. That's why bits of his writing are highlighted throughout these pages. To my ear, no poet captures the richness of rural Galloway life and the musicality of the Scots language quite like Burns.

DOWNHILL FROM HERE

We're heading southeast now on the A76, a pleasant two-lane highway. Though the *A* designation means it's a main route, traffic is sparse this morning. Thanks to temperate weather, Scottish roads are generally in good repair; even the less-traveled B roads (my favorites) are well maintained, though on some of the minor routes we're more likely to encounter a herd of cattle or a flock of sheep than another car.

Sea gulls cover the fields like low-growing cotton plants, while large clumps of rosebay willowherb line the road. Bright green, slender leaves march up the long stalks toward rosy pink blossoms at the top, which will bloom again at summer's end.

Rumble strips along the edge of the road alert me when I drift too far left. American drivers must be easy to spot: we're the ones using turn signals. Not that we use them at home. But here, turn signals serve a dual purpose: to remind us what we're doing ("Bear left, Liz. No, *left.*") and to warn other drivers, "Tourist behind the wheel. Take cover."

Surely we give ourselves away consulting a map the size of a tablecloth in a car the size of a breadbox. Can you tell from the Travelmaster what we're crossing just now? Cessnock Water. *Hmm.* Not nearly as romantic sounding as the River Doon to our west, scene of the Brig o' Doon made famous in the Burns poem "Tam o' Shanter." Built in the fifteenth century, the famous bridge affords a lovely view of the Doon and the gentle hills that surround its banks.

> The sun was nearing its zenith when they descended
> into a wooded valley and crossed the River Doon over
> an old sandstone bridge. Its single, high arch spanned
> the placid waters below and carried them into the village of Alloway.
>
> *Grace in Thine Eyes*

Alas, we'll not have time for historic Alloway on this trip nor for neighboring Ayr, much as I admire that seaside town, nor for the Isle of Arran with its majestic profile rising from the Firth of Clyde like a sleeping warrior. Tell yourself, as I always do, "Next time." Because there *will* be a next time; the edge-of-town signs insist upon it: "Haste Ye Back."

In truth, few signs clutter the landscape. Motorways feature a small number out of necessity. Yield when you see "Give Way," pay attention if a simple "!" alerts you to trouble on the road ahead, and look for a "Refuse Tip" to deposit your trash. Otherwise, once you've turned onto a given route, it's assumed you know where you're going.

A FINE PROSPECT

Without billboards to mar the view and with relatively few trees covering the land, we're presented with an uninterrupted vista. It's only fitting that

Scotland is the home of golf, since the countryside looks like an endless fairway, the acres of green neatly groomed by sheep. Wildflowers brighten the hedgerows—red campion, with its deep pink petals, and sunny yellow buttercups—and across the ground lies a blanket of lavender clover.

Especially on a morning like this, the view in all directions is breathtaking. Beyond the outskirts of Mauchline, the rolling farmland unfurls in smoother waves than we'll find farther south in Galloway, where rocks stud the landscape. Here leafy hedgerows rather than stone fences divide the pastures.

Och! I spoke too soon. There's a ribbon of stone running along the boundary of that farm, keeping the ewes and their lambs from wandering onto the roadway.

We call them stone fences in Kentucky, but here they're *dykes,* made from rocks found amid the streams and fields. Nothing holds the stones in place except gravity and the skill of the builder, yet many dykes have withstood two centuries of storms. I love the sight of them crisscrossing the farmlands like gray charcoal lines drawn by the Master's hand.

They had the narrow country road to themselves, the
edges lined with *dry stane dykes*—stone fences fitted
together without mortar—and beyond them, grazing
sheep. Bits of wool caught on the lower branches of the
shrubs, giving the bushes and hedgerows fleecy skirts.

Whence Came a Prince

Curling through New Cumnock, where "Flow gently, sweet Afton"
appears on the village sign, we cross said Afton twice. Soon we're surrounded by countryside again, with an expansive view of patchwork farms
stitched in green and gold. Mountains rise all around us—the bald
Lowther Hills due east, round-shouldered Blackcraig Hill to the south—
as we enter the region officially known as Dumfries and Galloway, com-
prised of the old counties of Dumfriesshire, Kirkcudbrightshire, and
Wigtownshire. That is to say, *home.*

Already the terrain looks different. Greener, if that's possible, and
plush, like wide-wale corduroy. The roll of the land has increased, pitching
and turning constantly. Up and down we go, following the River Nith on
its meandering course through the valley, passing through sleepy Kirkconnel
and continuing downhill.

A van parked by the road gives us pause with its curious list of services:
"Dry Rot, Wet Rot, Rising Damp, Woodworm." Though they sound like
characters from a Tolkien novel—Elfwine, Forlong, and Wormtongue
would fit right in—they are in fact maladies common to British homes. We
also pass an auto-body-repair shop that advertises *panel beating,* with roadside assistance provided by a *breakdown service.* I, for one, pray our hired
car will return to Glasgow unbeaten and unbroken.

We're approaching Sanquhar now, a place more easily said—
"SANK-er"—than spelled. That's the parish church on the rise overlooking the Sanquhar Academy athletic field. A royal burgh from
centuries past when the crown bestowed such honors, elevating a village
to market-town status and granting it certain legal privileges, Sanquhar
boasts an impressive *tolbooth*. The cupola-topped building was erected in
1735 to serve as both town hall and prison, though folk seldom remained
behind bars for long. Murderers were summarily hanged, witches stran-
gled. Lesser criminals were fined, banished, whipped through the town,
branded with a hot iron, or nailed by the ear to the gallows. Cheery, eh?

Within the burgh we'll find our first castle and a post office in con-
tinual use since 1712, earning it the designation "Oldest Working Post
Office in the World." That's right…the *world*.

But it's not stamps you'll be wanting at this hour; it's something to
eat, aye?

SECOND BREAKFAST

An' cheese an' bread, frae women's laps,

Was dealt about in lunches.

ROBERT BURNS

*H*ere's a likely place for a meal: Burnside Tearoom on the threshold of Sanquhar. For the moment, put aside any notions of lace curtains, flowered wallpaper, fine china, sterling silver, and ruffled aprons. A typical Scottish tearoom, Burnside combines several businesses in one: a Thames Petrol station, a jet wash for self-service car cleaning, a convenience store with flats of pansies out front, and, as promised, a tearoom.

Local residents bustle in and out with takeaway bags as we sit at one of a dozen tables in this plain but tidy restaurant. Nearby, a mother tends her young charge, strapped in a stroller, while a gathering of older gents hunker over empty coffee cups.

We study the menu, surprised at the variety of offerings. At ten in the morning anything goes: savory or sweet, choose your fancy. Will it be *prawn* cocktail—we'd call them shrimp—or beans on toast? Hot filled rolls, like a hamburger, or oven-baked jacket potatoes stuffed with cheese? What about peach melba or a toasted teacake smothered in butter?

A savory, a sweet, *and* a pot of tea, you say? Well done.

Don't look now, but a wee *brownie* has spotted us. Three years old at the most, with copper-tinted hair and an elfin smile, she clings to her mother's flowered skirts even as her wide, brown eyes assess the two strangers who've invaded her neighborhood eatery. When I wink at her, she hides her face, suddenly shy.

Here comes our morning repast. Some might call it *elevenses,* though we're an hour ahead of schedule and enjoying more than coffee and a biscuit. Have a stab at my sausage roll while I pour my tea.

Though I like cream in my coffee, I never thought I'd favor milk in my tea. "Dishwater," my husband calls it, rolling his eyes. The secret is a really strong brew, which I discovered the day I dunked an Earl Grey tea bag in a Thermos of boiling hot water, screwed on the cap, then forgot about it *for an hour.* The tea was still hot but black as ink. Rather than waste it, I topped my steaming cup with whole milk. The fragrant richness of the tea and the creamy smoothness of the milk... Well, what can I say? Love at first sip.

GHOSTIES AND BEASTIES

Energy restored and stomachs sated, we climb into our car, briefly consult Landranger Map 78, then continue southeast through Sanquhar, where two-story houses in brown, tan, and ivory crowd both sides of the street, their front doors opening directly onto the narrow sidewalks. A sign advertising a local band, the Ghosties, catches my eye—

Ack! I hit the brakes as the High Street narrows to a single lane, skirting the dominant stone tolbooth. When the road widens to two lanes, I sneak a quick glance at the historic site in my rearview mirror, admiring the wrought-iron railing on the double staircase that climbs up to the door on one side and down to the street on the other.

Intrigued by various store signs—"Fruiter" suggests fresh produce and "Snap Lab" indicates photo developing—we nearly miss the Oldest Post Office in the World. Painted white with black trim and brick red doors, the building is distinguished from its neighbors only by the "1712" above the left entrance. A long row of one-story cottages leads to the edge of town, where Castleview Service Station reminds us to look south toward a neglected ruin with a dark history despite its pastoral setting.

A tall, crumbling tower and a stony stretch of wall with gaping windows—that's what's left of Sanquhar Castle, built by the Crichton family, then abandoned by later owners for the far grander Drumlanrig Castle to the south. Legend says the castle is guarded by a "White Lady"—in this case, the ghost of Marion of Dalpeddar, a fair-haired lass from the neighborhood who disappeared in 1590. Murdered by one of the Crichtons, the story goes.

To my way of thinking, the only frightening aspect of Sanquhar Castle is the real danger of breaking your neck while clambering about the toppled walls. Perhaps that's why no signs point the way to the ruinous keep encouraging tourists to investigate further. Sturdier castles await us, though this one still charms from a distance.

Nestled in a valley with sheep-covered hills rising on both sides, we're surrounded by all that defines Dumfries and Galloway: a faint mist on the hilltops; impossibly green grass; *whinstone* dykes tracing the *marches,* or boundary lines; and whitewashed houses. Usually built of stone, often *harled,* or roughcast with lime and small stones, most farmhouses are unadorned. Shutters are absent, doorways are plain, and landscaping is limited to whatever trees the Lord chose to plant.

Each property boasts a distinctive name, the sort one might give a thoroughbred racehorse—Twentyshilling, Glengenny, Coshogle, Sweetbit—though we'll rarely see a family surname at the gate. Often there's laundry flapping on the lines but not on Sunday; even in the twenty-first century, Sabbath observances linger. Those animals with the large, shaggy feet are Shire horses, a popular British breed. Border collies are a common sight as well, easily recognized by their black-and-white coats and their confident trot.

Lower the windows, and you'll hear a soundtrack far more soothing than the Celtic harp music that lilts from our CD player: the faint bleating of sheep.

WOULD EWE LOOK AT THAT!

Cows don't make people go, "Ohhh, look." But sheep do. Something about the softness of their fleece or the roundness of their bodies has a winsome appeal. Sheep have inspired poets and artists for centuries. Think of Walbourn's golden-hued *Bringing Home the Sheep* or Rossetti's tender Victorian verse, "If I were a shepherd, I would bring a lamb." A flock of sheep moving as one, guided by their shepherd, is a fair sight to behold.

> Flocks of blackface sheep stood about on both sides of
> the road, heads bent to the ground, horns curved about
> their ears. They were evenly scattered as though carefully
> placed by a shepherd making good use of his master's
> grazing land.
>
> *Thorn in My Heart*

Most of the time sheep prefer to stand in one spot, heads bowed, nibbling grass. Now and again they settle down for a nap, but the rest of the time they're eating, propped on spindly legs that don't look stout enough to support their abundant bodies. "Lawn mowers," one Dumfriesshire farmer called them. Every fortnight collies must move the sheep to another pasture lest the flock eat the grass down to the roots.

We'll see all manner of sheep in Galloway: white, off-white, gray, tan, gold, brown, black, solid, and spotted. Different breeds mingle on the hills, some with pointy noises and perky ears, others with gray and white mottled faces. Not all sheep with black faces are blackface sheep, however. When I included on my Web site a photo with the caption "Blackface sheep," a member of the Blackface Sheep Breeders' Association kindly corrected me. The caption now reads "Scottish sheep." Seemed safe.

Sheep also come in red, green, and blue, though not naturally so. Farmers spray-paint their sheep to keep track of them, like branding cattle. When my husband first saw a fluorescent red blob decorating a sheep's shoulder, he feared it might be the work of young hooligans with too much time (and paint) on their hands. Sheep vandalism, if you will. But no, it's a *keel* mark, scrubbed clean when sheep and fleece part company in June.

Lambs, traditionally born at Eastertide, are reason enough to visit Scotland in the spring. On their tottery legs with their sweet faces and still-white fleece, newborn lambs engender a feeling of protectiveness; they clearly need a mother to feed them and a shepherd to guide them. Indeed, don't we all?

One blue-sky morning while driving across Galloway, I came over a rise to find two lambs in the middle of the road, nursing. The ewe had her feet well planted, and her offspring seemed most intent on having their breakfast. Nothing to do but put the car in park, lower the windows, drink in the sweet spring air, and admire the endearing scene before me.

Those are the Scottish memories I most cherish. Not walking the bustling streets of old Edinburgh or gazing at the stained-glass windows of Glasgow Cathedral but spending a halcyon moment on a lone country road with a patient ewe and her *twa* lambs.

TO KIRK WE GO

I'll get my Sunday's sark on,
An' meet you on the holy spot.

ROBERT BURNS

*H*aving insisted that no one ever slows down to gaze at cows, I
am doing precisely that, easing my foot off the gas pedal as we
approach a herd of dairy cattle in chocolate brown and creamy white.
They look unusually clean, as if they'd been washed and scrubbed on the
Sabbath eve, ready for *kirk* in the morning.

Some herds have shiny chestnut coats; others are blond and huge.
Galloway cattle, as they're known, are much larger than other cattle and
hornless with "rough, glossy, black coats,"[1] as Rev. Dick describes them.
My favorite cows are a black-and-white breed, affectionately known as
belties. As the name suggests, they have a wide white band around their

middles, with solid black fore and aft. Plush-toy belties are a standard feature at tourist gift shops, but only real ones bring a smile to my face. I realize they're cows, but you must admit they're appealing.

The hills on the east side are growing steeper, closing us in. I find their nearness comforting, like having the folds of a wool blanket tucked around my shoulders. Our map provides their colorful names—Meikle Snout, Threehope Height, and Cold Moss, the last topping two thousand feet. Wanlockhead, the highest village in all Scotland, sits among them, dispelling any misconceptions of the Lowlands being low. The Mennock Pass, an eye-opening drive through glacier-carved hills, is a tempting diversion, but suppose we press on. It *is* Sunday and nearing eleven, when most parish churches open their doors for an hour of worship.

No church spires are in sight just now, only stands of larch in unnaturally straight rows, courtesy of the Forestry Commission. A roadside sign explains: "The South West Scotland climate is more favorable for the rapid growth of quality conifers than anywhere in Europe." And here they are, rapidly growing on both sides of the A76. A morning breeze stirs the branches, making them dance and wave. The bright green needles look especially vivid against the darkening pewter skies.

I seldom study the heavens at home, certain what I'll find: solid blue, pale gray, or endless clouds. In Scotland, I can't take my eyes off the shifting moods and watercolor tints above me. Though the sun was shining when we left Sanquhar twenty minutes ago, the skies have grown rather ominous, with only a few blue patches remaining—"enough to make a sailor's *sark*," the old saying goes.

Perhaps because this is an island or because it's as far north as, say, Ketchikan, Alaska, the weather changes quickly here. And the sky feels closer to the ground—mere sensation, mind you, not scientific fact—as if we could stand on a ladder and touch those thick, gray clouds looming over the road. If you're game to try, we'd better hurry; clouds have a way of disappearing without a by-your-leave. I once heard a Scottish weather forecaster describe the outlook as "continuing changeable." Exactly so.

We're heading due south now, though not for long. I've a parish church in mind for our Sunday service, which will require a bit of back-tracking. At the sign for Carronbridge, we'll bear northeast on the A702, one of the more beguiling stretches of road in Dumfriesshire. How could it not be when it leads to a place called Elvanfoot? At first we're hemmed in by forested road, but around the bend we discover a massive semicircle of mountains in the near distance.

Roman soldiers traversed this valley two millenniums ago, leaving behind the ruins of a fortlet. (Though it sounds like something you'd serve for breakfast, a fortlet garrisoned no more than eighty soldiers.) Farther north can be found the steep, green slopes of the Dalveen Pass. According to our map, here's the first yellow road on our trip: less than four meters wide, no route number, no white line painted down the center, and no shoulder. Only the Durisdeer signpost assures us we're turning in the right direction as we plunge down this steep track, past a herd of cows, then over a narrow bridge.

After a few harrowing turns on blind curves, the road stretches before us in one long, undulating line, drawn by a steady hand through hilly pastures. Except for a few birds on the wing, the countryside is utterly still, as if awed by the mountains, as we are. In the foothills rises a square church tower, surrounded by trees and gray-roofed white cottages. I found Durisdeer listed in my *Churches to Visit in Scotland* guide; now we'll see if it's truly "unspoilt" and "peaceful,"[2] as the author claims.

Wooden Pews and Marble Columns

The cluster of cottages lining the village square hardly prepares us for the impressive church that dominates this forgotten hamlet at road's end. Plain yet elegant windows march down one pink-hued exterior wall, while arched Palladian windows decorate the other. Such grandeur is easily explained. Three centuries ago, when every resident of Durisdeer Parish was expected to attend Sunday services, the Duke of Queensberry, patron of the parish, built the church to his own high standards, including ducal retiring rooms to accommodate his retinue.

We park our car where His Grace's horses might once have grazed, then venture inside. White walls make the most of available light, and a length of red carpet softens our steps. In addition to open rows of pews turned toward the pulpit, we find pairs of long benches of yellow pine facing each other across narrow tables and enclosed in waist-high wooden boxes. Here and there, initials are carelessly carved into the soft wood, and threadbare red cushions line the benches. Are all these well-worn box pews spoken for, claimed by Durisdeer parishioners for generations? Or may we choose one and slip inside?

After standing around, feeling like…well, tourists, we approach an older woman in a blue and white checked dress, sitting alone. "Beg pardon, ma'am."

She peers at us over her shoulder. "Ye may sit wherever ye like. Though not here, if ye *dinna* mind. *Ma* family's due shortly." Her matter-of-fact tone is tempered by a faint smile; we are welcome, it seems.

According to the sign posted at the entrance, worship begins at 11:45, which can only mean one thing: Rev. James Scott preaches in another village before he conducts the service here. That's the way of things in modern rural parishes, where offering plates are as empty as the pews. Church of Scotland ministers are often assigned to more than one congregation by the presbytery, juggling two services in two places on a given morning, or alternating services from one week to the next. One Sunday I visited four Galloway churches before I found one with its doors open. Heartbreaking, in a country where religion once held such sway.

But small does not mean lifeless. Parishioners of all ages begin arriving as we tentatively claim a pew, prepared to relocate at the first furrowed brow. Though the hymnary contains no notes—only words to the psalms, paraphrases, and hymns—the small pipe organ looks promising. Two remnants from the eighteenth century decorate the pulpit: a pewter baptismal basin and a sandglass to mark the hour-long sermons of old. The view through the clear glass windows is appropriately pastoral. Solemn rows of gravestones surround the church, inspiring a sense of the eternal and a measure of reverence.

I bow my head to pray and reach for your hand, as I do my husband's on Sunday mornings, remembering the biblical promise: "For where two or three come together in my name, there am I with them."[3] And the Lord *is* with us, whether we're flying across the ocean or gazing out the windows of our hired car or sitting on a hard, wooden pew. Prayer connects us to this setting, this congregation. The unfamiliar becomes familiar. Though I don't move my lips, I know my prayerful thoughts have been heard.

When I lift my head and open my eyes, squeezing your hand before I let go, I find you are smiling as well.

Home, home, home. Never more so than in this place, in this hour.

Rev. Scott climbs into the pulpit as he has done for many decades, it appears. Age has whitened his hair but not bent his tall frame. Kindness shines from his countenance. By now, thirty or so people have gathered for worship. Tender-eyed mums and stoic dads, wiggly offspring and saintly grandmothers—all have found their seats. Though they take turns looking us over, their faces are friendly, their manners polite. In 1791, Durisdeer's minister called his parishioners "hospitable, honest, sober, and industrious" and "of the middle size."[4] I'm not sure about their relative stature, but the praiseworthy character of the people seems intact.

We have no printed bulletin in hand to guide us through the worship service, no posted list of hymns, so we do our best to follow along. Not knowing the tunes, we keep our voices low. Even so, a freckle-faced lad turns and grins at us each time we sing a wrong note. After delivering a short but heartfelt sermon from the gospel of John, Rev. Scott offers a gentle benediction.

Duly dismissed, the congregation begins moving into the aisles, exchanging warm greetings. "Are ye staying in the neighborhood?" our blue-checked older woman inquires as she follows us toward the doorway, where Rev. Scott stands bidding his flock farewell.

"We're lodging in Kirkbean," I tell her.

Her eyes widen. "So far as that?"

It's a cliché worth repeating: in the United States, one hundred years is a long time; in the United Kingdom, one hundred miles is a long distance. Though our hotel is an easy thirty-mile drive south of here, that sounds far indeed to folk who are accustomed to walking around the corner for a sack of groceries or a pint of Tennent's lager.

"Might ye come again next Sunday for our spring communion?" she asks. "One o' the elders can give ye a card, if ye like."

As she motions a gray-haired gentleman to her side, I apologize and explain we'll be visiting elsewhere.

"I see." Her eyes narrow a bit, as if we're church hoppers, deciding which parish has the most comfortable pews. "Before ye leave, dinna miss the Queensberry Aisle." She nods toward the northeast corner of the church, then ambles off with a wave of her hand.

I call out my thanks, glad to have directions to a separate but attached building, which contains what the guidebook termed a "most amazing monument."[5] Circling around the right side of the church, we find a plain entrance, unmarked and unlocked. The enormous door creaks open, and a musty smell wafts out to greet us. When we step inside the mausoleum, the cooler air makes me shiver. Or perhaps it's the overwhelming amount of marble—floor tiles in black and cream squares, intricately carved pillars, trumpeting angels, an immense white marble canopy, and a reclining duke and duchess—all in the baroque style. That is to say, vastly and delightfully overdone, a remnant of the medieval church that once stood here and a fitting shrine to the aristocrat whose silver built the present sanctuary.

Even with a large window ushering in what natural light the day has to offer, the aisle is bathed in shadows, dispelled only by the flash of our cameras. I catch myself tiptoeing across the floor as if the marbleized second Duke of Queensberry might uncross his legs and rise at any moment. I don't truly exhale until we're headed to the car.

Almost There

With Durisdeer in our rearview mirror, we're headed south toward Dumfries, but first we've one more quaint spot to pass through. The name alone sent me looking for this village a decade ago: Thornhill. Perhaps a striking hawthorn once grew on this high ridge long before the cross streets were paved and coaching inns built. Thornhill was laid out by the first Duke of Queensberry—rather poorly, according to Dorothy Wordsworth, sister to the famous poet, who called the cottages "so small that they might have been built to stamp a character of insolent pride on his own huge mansion of Drumlanrig."[6] True, Drumlanrig is enormous, with its baroque excesses. And the whitewashed cottages lining the streets are indeed humble, without flower boxes or painted shutters to brighten the look of them.

Yet that's the Scotland I love: straightforward, without pretense. Barren, wind-swept hills stir my soul far more than manicured lawns. A wee cottage made of rubble, not a mansion filled with marble, fairly warms my heart. And so the thoroughfare of Thornhill, with unadorned homes and shops, suits me perfectly.

Drumlanrig Street skirts the *mercat* cross at the center of the village, where markets and fairs were once held. A fine old hotel, the red sandstone Buccleuch & Queensberry is bedecked with flowers and has its doors propped open, inviting our custom. I've not stepped inside any of Thornhill's inns or pubs, but Robert Burns did so frequently, fulfilling his duties as an excise officer, in charge of determining that spirits were legally obtained and severely taxed—a curious day job for a plowman turned poet. We'll wave at his farm a bit farther down the A76.

Though the day is young, our brief night's sleep is catching up with me. What about a fresh pot of tea when we reach Dumfries? Or we could pop into that restaurant to our left, where my husband and I once shared a meal. Oh, the things we learned! My cola was served cold but without ice, and Bill's royal coffee was topped with whipped cream. I ordered a ham *toastie*, made with thin-sliced ham and black pickled something. Snail, maybe. *Ick*. Bill's cheese toastie was a traditional toasted cheese sandwich but with limp circles of half-cooked onion inside.

You'd rather wait for tea until we reach Dumfries? A wise decision.

Not far south of Thornhill we pass through the hamlet of Closeburn, where Rev. Scott preached earlier this morning. Remarkable to think of an octogenarian making such an effort every Sunday. Yet didn't we pass a trio of cyclists—every one of them over seventy years old—headed for the hills, dressed in the latest biking gear?

The way I see it, Scots are walkers, climbers, and hikers, born in a country made for exploring on foot, which they do from an early age until, like Enoch, they at last walk with God.[7]

A fine plan, really, should we ever choose to get out of the car.

COUNTRY AND TOWN

Upon a simmer Sunday morn,
When Nature's face is fair.

ROBERT BURNS

*T*he River Nith has widened considerably now, inviting anglers to test her waters. A stoop-shouldered man in a red plaid shirt and mud-colored waders casts his line over the water, perhaps hoping to tote home a salmon or trout for his Sunday dinner. Hanging laundry on the Sabbath may be frowned upon, but fishing is always apropos.

We pass a signpost for Ae, reputed to be the shortest toponym in the U.K. The village must be small as well—we're hard pressed to find it on the map—but the Forest of Ae covers 5,500 acres, much of it those fast-growing conifers. The hills are lower and rounder now, though no less pleasing to eye or ear; Fleuchlarg and Clauchrie and Barnmuir and Mullach rest deep in your throat, requiring a trill of the tongue to get them out.

A road sign alerting us to watch for deer has us scanning the edges of the forest, though it's not a deer-y time of day; the gloaming is when we're likely to spot roe deer.

Gloaming. Lovely word, isn't it? Old English for *twilight,* that languid hour when the sky takes on a rosy afterglow and the wispy clouds, a tinge of blue. Sounds and voices become muted as the earth exhales, releasing a faint mist into the cooler evening air.

> The last hour before darkness was Jamie's favorite, particularly in the summer. He stood on the lawn, watching the sunset paint the sky in colors only the Almighty could name. After singing all evening, the birds had grown quieter, making way for the tawny owls to take their turn.
>
> *Whence Came a Prince*

During the gloaming in Scotland, time stretches beyond its confines. The brightly hued sky fades ever so gradually to gray, then to deep blue, then after a lengthy pause to black. When darkness finally comes on a summer eve, it's unexpected, as if the world were meant to remain bathed in perpetual twilight.

After a few long-lit evenings in Galloway, I predict you'll fall beneath the gloaming's spell, as I always do, finding some excuse to wander outdoors after supper and gaze at the darkening sky until the first star blinks into view.

Come nightfall, a host of beasties appear: stripe-faced badgers and prickly hedgehogs; red foxes, with their small ears and silky tails; weasels and stoats, odd creatures with long, reddish brown bodies and small heads. Time to retreat indoors and leave the woods and gardens to them.

We're driving through Auldgirth now, a fine name for a wee place. *Auld* is the Scots word for old, and *girth* means a place of sanctuary. (Granted, another definition is corpulent, but surely the early settlers didn't name their village old and fat!) Auldgirth spans the A76, with a grocery store on the right and the Auldgirth Inn off to the left.

A bit farther down is Friars Carse Country House Hotel, built in 1773. Though all we see from the road is an inviting sign, we can visualize the setting: *carse* means low-lying land along a river. Captain Robert Riddell, Burns's neighbor and friend, lived at Friars Carse and gave the poet a key to the Hermitage, a little summerhouse on the property.

Regrettably, their friendship was strained to the breaking point one cold December night. After a tastelessly staged romp, fueled by too many glasses of port and inspired by one of the myths involving the founding of Rome—the Rape of the Sabines—Burns was banished from the Riddell home in disgrace.

Now *this* is why history fascinates me. Forget those boring lists of names, dates, and political skirmishes from our high-school textbooks; people and their stories are the fabric of history. When we begin to pluck apart that tightly woven cloth, what vivid threads we find!

The village of Dunscore, home to feisty-though-fictional Jane Grierson, lies to our west, and here's Ellisland Farm, once home to the Burns family, who also worshiped in Dunscore. Suppose we pay a visit to Ellisland on our return trip north? At the moment, I'm hoping a fresh pot of Earl Grey is brewing in Dumfries.

DISC DRIVE

It's not your imagination: my hands *are* gripping the steering wheel more firmly. With a population topping thirty-five thousand, Dumfries boasts sufficient traffic to merit a driver's keen attention, plus enough *vennels,* or alleys, and one-way streets to thoroughly confuse a novice.

Fear not, for I've learned the secret of driving in Dumfries: park the car.

First we'll go over the river—aye, the Nith again—and through the pedestrian crowd, then dart down the east bank on a street that has the audacity to change names three times in as many blocks. Park Lane becomes Brewery Street becomes Whitesands, where horses, sheep, and cattle were sold on fair days of old. Since then, they've paved paradise and put up a car park. The three-hour limit is a nuisance, but the price is right: one cardboard disc.

Freely obtained from any nearby merchant, the blue and white disc lets us park in a disc zone, spin the notched wheel to our arrival time, then display the disc between dashboard and windshield. Let me worry about locking up the car while you admire the red sandstone bridge and the white swans gliding along the riverbank. At the far end of the span, you'll see the Old Bridge House, dating from 1660. It was an inn, among other things, and can rightly claim, "Burns slept here."

By all means, dig out your camera, though you can be sure those six graceful arches will still be here when we return. Devorgilla Bridge— named for Lady Devorgilla, mother of John Balliol, short-lived king of Scotland—has been standing since 1431, spanning the Nith between Whitesands and Brigend, a rough settlement once favored by lawless *gaberlunzies* looking to steal a man's silver.

AULD LANG SYNE

"Shall I snap yer picture?"

A gentleman of advanced age steps forward, his gray shirt and trousers neatly pressed, the corduroy cap on his head covering what's left of his reddish brown hair. When he doffs said cap and smiles, we hand over our Pentax and Sony, convinced by the twinkle in his eye that his offer is genuine and not a ploy to pocket our cameras.

We pose by the steps to the old bridge in true tourist fashion as he takes one photo, then another, chatting us up all the while, like a dentist asking questions while his patient's mouth is full of cotton.

"Ye're from the States, then? On holiday? 'Tis grand weather now the sun's out. Have ye been in Dumfries *lang*?"

We can neither nod nor answer until our photography session is done, at which point we confess we are indeed Americans on a tour of Dumfries and Galloway.

"Are ye now?" He beams at us, clearly pleased with our choice.

As we retrieve our cameras and bid him farewell, we set our sights on tea and perhaps something more substantial to restore our flagging energy. The first day abroad is the hardest. Back home, our families are probably leaning on the open fridge door, thinking about breakfast. We should call them now that they're up. Keep an eye out for a phone box, though the classic red ones are becoming scarce as they are replaced by drab glass models with a big *BT* (British Telecom) on the side. Aye, the phone will still take your coins but without providing a nice photo op in return.

Crossing Whitesands, I admire the hodgepodge of brick and sandstone buildings clustered all in a row. Three and four stories tall, many with steep roofs and dormer windows, the shops and houses exude a comfortable air. Neither pretentious nor dowdy, Dumfries is a place one could easily live, a place John Wesley called "the neatest as well as the most civilised town that I have seen in the Kingdom."[1] And *he* was from England.

Friars Vennel will carry us up to the High Street—and I do mean *up*. Bit of a climb. Forgive my huffing and puffing. Farther down the Nith, the land broadens into mud flats where the river meets the sea, but here the water carves its way through hillier ground, as your lungs will quickly demonstrate. It rained this morning; the paved brick surface is slick, and a few puddles remain as we cross Irish Street, where fashionable gentlemen of the eighteenth century built their town houses, extending the gardens down to the Nith's fertile banks.

As in most medieval burghs, the town center of Dumfries displays no apparent street plan. Streets no wider than a single car shoot off in odd directions; roads converge, then end abruptly; a town map answers only so many questions. We delight in poking about here and there, observing eight centuries of a work in progress. If we follow Greyfriars Street—so narrow the Dumfries Street Guide uses the slenderest arrow to point it out—we'll be standing near the spot where Robert the Bruce murdered his nemesis, John "the Red" Comyn, in February 1306 and so cleared the path to the throne of Scotland. Those are truly the days of auld lang *syne*, my dear.

The High Street has a smart look to it. Mansard roofs and well-dressed windows gaze down on the pedestrian thoroughfare, cars having been diverted elsewhere. The Midsteeple, built three hundred years ago to house various council offices, rises from the town center. Three stories of red sandstone boast a fine clock, a white cupola, and an outside stair leading up to the first floor. Well, Americans would call it the second floor, but here it's the first floor, while our first floor is their ground floor. Still with me?

Along with the soundtrack the sea gulls provide, fiddle music floats across the pedestrian square. In the shadow of the Midsteeple a woman in her forties offers a spirited rendition of a Burns tune—"My Love, She's but a Lassie Yet"—while her dog rests at her feet, keeping watch over the open fiddle case and its few coins. We stop to listen for a moment, then smile and add our silver to her meager earnings, hoping others will do the same.

Boots the Chemist, with its bright white exterior and familiar blue oval above the door, is a welcome sight. If we unpack tonight and realize we've forgotten some vital toiletry, this British gem among drugstores will save the day. I once enjoyed high tea with a friend in Edinburgh, courtesy of Boots and our hotel-room teapot. She brought a sack full of sandwich halves from a nearby Boots—egg mayonnaise (like egg salad, only more yellow), prawn and watercress, cheese and onion, bacon and bleu cheese—then cut them into dainty triangles and served them on plates borrowed from our breakfast cart. With our piping hot tea and shortbread rounds, we cozied up to our window overlooking Princes Street and watched the last rays of the winter sun disappear below the cityscape—at 3:30 in the afternoon.

There's the Hole i' the Wa' Inn, where Burns was known to bend his elbow. We'd have to duck through this murky, narrow *close*—a passageway between two buildings—to get a good look at the inn itself. The gold lettering on the black sign above the entranceway appears new. The inn, however, is not: "Est. 1620." I had a credible plate of pub food on my last visit here, and they certainly serve tea. But if you'll not mind walking a bit farther, we'll find an even older inn where Robert Burns also drank. And slept.

BURNS SLEPT HERE...
AND HERE

My name is Fun—your cronie dear
The nearest friend ye hae.

ROBERT BURNS

*T*hough he lived in Dumfries only the last five years of his short life, his face is everywhere—on signs and placards, on books and postcards—often reduced to a black-and-white profile, which vaguely resembles Alexander Nasmyth's famous portrait hanging in Edinburgh.

No matter. We know what the poet's image signifies: Robert Burns lived, wrote, loved, drank, supped...aye, and slept here.

And especially *here,* at the Globe Inn. I missed the place altogether the first time I strolled along the High Street. Two blocks down from the Midsteeple, the Globe is squeezed between a glass-fronted charity shop and a

Subway restaurant. A wooden doorframe surrounds the entrance to a white-painted close, with all the particulars lettered on the wide frame: "Est. 1610." Older than the Hole i' the Wa' by a decade. "Burns Howff." A fine Scots word meaning a favorite haunt. And bar lunches are served until 3:00.

Down the narrow close we stroll, glad the sun has returned to light our way. A hand-lettered sign—"The Globe"—looks Elizabethan with its elaborate gold *T* and *G*. One of the skinny twin doors (will we fit through?) stands ajar. Enticing aromas waft out to greet us: lamb, potatoes, sausage, curry, tea.

I'm in.

> A steep, narrow stair rose before them. Two sizable
> rooms to the left were spilling over with patrons
> and ale.
>
> *Thorn in My Heart*

Those red-carpeted steps leading to the next floor beg to be climbed. Burns often lodged upstairs and scratched verses on the windowpanes with his ring, including a stanza of "Comin' Thro' the Rye." Try doing that at a Marriott, and see if you're invited back.

Burns also consorted with a barmaid here in the summer of 1790, producing a wee daughter whom his wife, Jean, blithely accepted into their family *nine days* before she gave birth to their son William. Perhaps we should have Jean's profile featured at every turn instead of her husband's, for she was surely the more virtuous of the two.

Before we're seated, take a gander at the snug bar, or *snuggery*, as folk once called it: a cozy space, frequented by Burns and his cronies, with barely enough room for two small tables, both vacant at the moment, and a bar made of gleaming wood. Harness and tack would have hung from the wooden walls in Burns's day, and the lounge bar to the right was once the stables.

We can't linger here at the door, so cramped is the passageway between one room and the next. Wonderful, isn't it? As if Robert himself might squeeze by at any moment.

"Table for lunch?" a young lass with faintly purple hair wants to know. A pint of ale in one hand, a damp rag in the other, she nods toward the room to our left, no larger than twenty feet square and *chockablock* with patrons.

When my son and I shared a meal here one chilly January day, he likened this room to the captain's quarters of an old ship with the dark wood slightly warped and the doorframes askew, as if time and seawater had taken their toll. A broad, stone hearth along the far wall still bears an iron *gallows* used for holding pots over the fire when this room was the kitchen. Smoked meat must have hung from the ceiling hooks above us. The floors are dark brown—after a few centuries of serving food, best not to know what's ground beneath our feet—and the windows have narrow sills and sixteen small panes trimmed in black.

We settle into our seats as large oval trays laden with food emerge from the nearby kitchen and go sailing over our heads. The servers don't miss a step, balancing drinks and dishes with aplomb. Having worked in restaurants in my youth, I eye the narrow gaps between tables, the low ceilings, the uneven floors, the jostling of shoulders as people come and go, and I vow to leave our waitress a sizable tip.

Pub Grub Is a Misnomer

Whatever you've heard or read about British food being bland and unimaginative, the Globe and I hope to convince you otherwise. Just look at the menu. Aye, fish and chips are standard pub fare, but here the fresh Solway haddock is flaky, not mushy, and perfectly seasoned, and the chips are thick slabs of real potato, fried to a crisp, golden brown. There's malt vinegar on the table, should you care for it, and a brown sauce that doesn't quite tempt me. Perhaps if they told me the flavor, I'd give it a go.

The sticky toffee pudding, on the other hand, is beyond resisting: a date-flavored sponge cake covered with a rich sauce made of double cream, vanilla, demerara sugar, and heaps of butter, then served warm with ice cream and, if you're throwing caution to the winds, heavy cream as well.

That's what I'm having. And a plate of haddock. And tea.

I realize we ate this morning, but that was hours ago. Second breakfast, remember? And this is so late a lunch as to qualify as afternoon tea.

The Scotch lamb in rosemary gravy, served with crusty bread, is it? Good choice.

Tea arrives even before we've tucked away our purses. "Earl Grey," our waitress announces. She's not seen her twentieth birthday, yet her hand is splayed across the bottom of the round bar tray with the skill of an NBA player palming a basketball. "Tea for ye as well, *mem.*" She deposits a teacup on the cork-bottomed place mat, then disappears behind the swinging door to the kitchen, giving us a brief glimpse into the workings of the place.

I bow over my cup, inhaling. The fragrant steam alone is enough to revive me. Suppose we borrow the Burns grace, "At the Globe Tavern," meant to be offered before meat—that is, before any meal, be it porridge or broth.

> O Lord, when hunger pinches sore,
> Do thou stand us in stead,
> And send us from thy bounteous store
> A tup or wether head!

Hold that last thought. Dining on the head of a *tup*, or ram—let alone that of a castrated male lamb, called a *wether*—sounds a bit desperate. As if the leg of mutton ran out on Friday, the *haggis* was stuffed and boiled on Saturday, and here's what's left for the Sabbath. *Ugh.*

It's rumored that Burns preferred plain foods and hated tarts and sweets. As for me, just deliver my pudding, and I'll be happy.

Our food is not long in coming, though we're duly entertained while we wait. A half-dozen young women at the table next to us are having a hen party and clucking louder by the minute, though it's a musical sort of cluck.

"Meg, ye *canna* be serious! He *didna* say that?"

"Ye're daft for puttin' up with him."

Dark-haired Meg shrugs. "Aye, but he puts up with me…"

At which point they all laugh, lifting their glasses to a lad we'll never meet.

The thick Scottish brogue of, say, Aberdeen is uncommon in Galloway. Here the phrases are more sung than spoken, and each sentence ends on a higher note than it began. If we say, "Fine weather today," our voices start at an even pitch, then drop off. But in the Lowlands the words swing up, like a question. "Fine weather today?" That's why the safest response is "Aye." To everything.

As I slide my spoon around the plate to catch every delicious drop of cream, I'm especially glad I said aye to this delightful pudding. Help yourself to a spoonful. See what I mean? *Mmm.* My mother told me the first words I said were "Mmm, mmm, good." If only Gerber made puréed sticky toffee pudding for babies…

With some reluctance, we depart the Globe, a single hour left on our parking meter. If we hurry, we can tour the Burns House, then move our car before it's ticketed, towed, or tossed in the Nith.

AND HE TRULY SLEPT HERE

When Robert Burns moved his family to this two-story house in May 1793, the street was known as Millbrae Vennel. Now—surprise—it's called Burns Street. Sea gulls swoop and cry overhead as we cross the smooth cobblestones, bound for the open door. A white tent sign bearing the familiar Burns profile leans against the front steps.

Are you growing accustomed to all the red sandstone? Here's more of the same, with the plainest of entrances, true to the eighteenth century. Nice to visit a museum that allows cameras. And free admission? Lead the way.

After the Globe, this parlor ceiling feels quite high. Stark white woodwork matches stark white walls. Wooden floors, neither stained nor painted, make every step a noisy one. The hearth is fitted for cooking with an iron gallows lined with *cruiks* to hold the pots. Smooth plaster walls in the parlor give way to rougher textured walls in the humble kitchen.

The austere furnishings suit a poet's resources: a corner cupboard, chairs without cushions to soften the hard seats, end tables, a three-legged *creepie* by the hearth. The little hand-penned notes tacked around the room are illuminating. Robert breakfasted at nine with his family and kept a book beside him at table. He worked in the forenoon and spent evenings with his children. His wife, Jean Armour Burns, was the first woman in Dumfries to own a gingham dress—perhaps a gift from her husband, trying to make amends.

We climb the stairs and find two bedrooms: a smaller one for the lads, the larger for Robert and Jean, with a cozy, if not claustrophobia-inducing, box bed. More primitive creepies, their round seats a foot above the floor, stand guard by the hearth. I can see the value of sitting so close to the fire; what I can't see is how a woman rose without losing her balance and igniting her skirts.

Adjoining the master bedroom is a writing office that can only be called tiny. The low doorway almost brushes the crown of my head. But four windows provide ample light, and Burns would have enjoyed the view of Dumfries. His excise earnings no doubt paid for the fine writing table on which three quills stand at attention. The hinged top closes to convert it to a table. Or, as any writer understands, to hide the messy contents should company come knocking.

When I visited Chawton, Jane Austen's house in Hampshire, and tarried by her writing table, I did the unthinkable: I ignored the Do Not Touch sign, and…well…I *touched.* Ever so briefly, ever so lightly.

Shhh. I'm doing it again. Though no sign forbids it, I'm sure touching the furnishings is not encouraged, and so I silently beg forgiveness even as I brush my fingertips along the polished edge of Burns's desk.

If we had the energy, there's yet another museum worth exploring in this town fondly known as "the Queen of the South." Judging by your bleary eyes and my dragging feet, we might want to save the Robert Burns Centre for next time and instead aim our hired car toward the hotel, day-dreaming about hot baths and cool sheets.

To the west side of the Nith we go, then south on the A710, my favorite route in Galloway because it takes me to New Abbey. Because it takes me home.

HOMEWARD BOUND

Oh I am come to the low Countrie,

Ochon, Ochon, Ochrie!

ROBERT BURNS

After tooling along a fairly straight road out of Dumfries, we make an abrupt right at a property called Nethertown, then cross a narrow bridge over Cargen Pow. A Scots word, *pow* means a slow-moving stream flowing through fertile marshland. "Ditch-like," the dictionary says,[1] but where's the charm in that?

A flat carse stretched to the east, hinting at the marshy
shores of the River Nith beyond it. To the west, the
land sloped upward to hills once covered with trees.

Thorn in My Heart

Another sharp turn lands us in the center of Islesteps. Unless we stop, this tiny community will come and go in a blink. If we were properly shod and not so tired, I'd suggest we take that path to the right, which leads to Saint Queran's Well, one of six hundred healing wells scattered about the country, though few remain intact. This one is little more than a circle of plain stones laid around a shaft of water that overflows into Crooks Pow, but it's old; when Saint Queran's was cleaned out in 1870, they dredged up coins from the reign of Elizabeth I.

For centuries the faithful made pilgrimages to such wells, seeking relief from their ailments. The waters were believed to be especially potent on quarter days: Candlemas, Beltane, Lammas, and Hallowmas. When Christianity came to Scotland, many of the wells were sanctified, appeasing those reluctant to let go of pagan practices, especially when their health was at stake. Old parish records from the late eighteenth century include a list of the deceased and their curious causes of death: consumption, wasting, palsy, hives, dropsy, the vaguely worded "decay of nature," and the brief explanation, "suddenly."

Not a cloud remains in the sky; only sunshine and an occasional black-headed gull. Quite a different landscape from the moody Lowther Hills earlier, though one significant hill dominates the rural scene: Criffel, a mound of granite rising like a knuckle at the edge of the Solway Firth. "Crow's hill," some say it means.[2] I cannot vouch for crows, but I do know Criffel offers a lovely backdrop for this corner of Dumfries and Galloway. On overcast days the mammoth hill appears blue, with clouds shrouding the summit. Today we find it covered in patches of green and purplish brown. Rough looking, like suede.

The slopes seem gradual enough, as if we might easily stroll to the top, but veteran walkers caution that since you begin at sea level, you'll climb every one of its 1,868 feet. Phrases like "long, steady, and relentless climb"[3] make me think twice, but the unobstructed views of the Solway coast and the Lakeland Fells in England suggest the effort is worthwhile. On a clear day you can't see forever, but from Criffel's summit you may see the Isle of Man to the far southwest and the Isle of Arran to the distant northwest. When the men of Galloway were called to arms, bale fires were lit on mountaintops, Criffel being foremost among them.

Mabie Forest, a favorite spot for mountain bikers, rises above the farmlands. The dark green canopy of trees arching over the paved road leading into the forest is difficult to resist. *Hot bath. Cool sheets.* Those promising thoughts keep my eyes on the road as I note the familiar property names in passing. Gillfoot, a lovely old farmhouse at the bottom of a hill, stands hard against the road. Soon we begin a steady climb toward Whinnyhill House, affording us a stunning view across the lower Nith Valley. As we pass Auchenfad, then Martingirth, brooding Criffel seems prepared to fall on us.

My heart rate quickens as Shambellie Wood closes us in on the right and Shambellie Grange on the left. *Not much farther.* Rev. Dick aptly described this stretch of road: "The trees are set so close together, and their upper branches are so interwoven, that the light is as dim as in a cathedral."[4] A stand of old Scotch pines guards the approach to New Abbey; a marker dates the planting at 1775. While the Colonists prepared to fight for independence from England, these seedlings were already sending down roots.

At last the oblong sign for New Abbey appears: black letters on a white background with rounded corners, the sort posted outside almost every village in Scotland. But this is the village where the fictional Leana McBride worshiped and her sister, Rose, flirted; where Jamie McKie courted both cousins in turn, and his uncle Lachlan meddled unceasingly; where Duncan and Neda Hastings cared for field and hearth, and Colin Elliot, the grocer, sold his goods.

Tears filled my eyes on the May afternoon I discovered New Abbey; today is no different.

Home.

> Leana never wearied of the journey, for the view
> changed with the seasons: wildflowers in spring, yellow
> whin in summer, scarlet rowan trees in autumn, holly
> berries in winter.
>
> *Thorn in My Heart*

I made five research trips to Dumfries and Galloway before I was certain what tales I was meant to tell. Even so, my frugal husband, who squeezes every penny and counts it twice, understood that I needed to go to Scotland, *had* to go, that a series of novels would follow someday, that experiencing the setting firsthand would help the stories come alive.

And so when I labor in my writing study, surrounded by memories of Newabbey (the eighteenth-century spelling), I effortlessly walk through the village, peer in cottage windows, tarry where the old kirk once stood, run barefoot through the pine forest, drink a handful of cool water from the burn, and sit beneath the abbey's red sandstone arches.

Because of a loving God and a generous husband, my heart can travel thousands of miles at the turn of a single page.

A SENSE OF PLACE

Stranger, go! Heav'n be thy guide!
Quod the Beadsman of Nithside.

ROBERT BURNS

*N*ow it's your turn to meet New Abbey. The fifty-pence drive-by tour comes first; the ten-quid walking tour comes tomorrow. The moment we cross the bridge, we're plunged into the heart of the village. Directly to our right is a corn mill, built at the end of the eighteenth century, though a mill has stood in the same spot for seven centuries. We'll get a closer look in the morning.

At the end of a tall hedgerow outlining the tight left curve appears a handsome, three-story building with gray granite exterior and gold lettering. The Abbey Arms was built in 1826 as a temperance inn—a well-maintained, closely regulated public house, which served food and coffee and encouraged temperate drinking habits. No word on how well they succeeded on that last bit.

My husband and I sat at a small table by the front window of the Abbey Arms for our first supper in Scotland. We enjoyed a local cheddar cheese, which was not especially sharp yet highly flavorful, and a Roquefort cheese that was crumbly yet creamy, served with a mackerel pâté and finely ground oatcakes. The soup was carrot and bean, with only a few butter beans but rich with seasoning. Dessert was Sweetheart shortbread, cut into heart shapes and served with fresh cream and juicy raspberries.

Some meals you never forget.

That's Criffel Inn on our left. The brown-on-white, half-timbered design and peaked roof remind me of Germany. I lodged at the inn once and created quite a stir when I requested a small bowl of currants at breakfast and promptly dumped them into my porridge. I've since learned there is a proper way to eat porridge, involving spoonfuls of hot oats and a cold glass of milk. Adding cinnamon, brown sugar, or raisins is strictly American style.

Next to the Criffel Inn you'll notice a craft shop–grocer–newsagent–post office. My husband's assessment of the place was "If Carberry's doesn't have it, you don't need it."

That's it for the business district until we reach Abbey Cottage, a tea-room and shop situated at the other end of things. New Abbey's narrow Main Street curves like the letter S, with cottages edging both sides. Though there are two lanes with a broken white line down the center, drivers don't have much room for error, nor do pedestrians since the road has no shoulder and no real sidewalks. But that's part of the village's charm: you cannot escape its embrace.

The minister of the parish wrote in 1790, "Newabbey is a pleasant village of 50 houses...surrounded with beautiful woods."[1] The numbers have climbed a bit since then, but otherwise little has changed. The woods are still beautiful, dark, and deep, and the village remains pleasant indeed. An occasional hanging flower basket adds a splash of color, and the stone cottages are neatly trimmed in light blue, dark red, or the perennial favorite, black.

ABBEY ROAD

I can tell by your awed expression you've glimpsed the sacred ruins that dominate the village. Sweetheart Abbey, founded in 1273, is new compared to Dundrennan Abbey, established eighteen miles southeast of here more than a century earlier; hence, the parish name of *New* Abbey. The central tower rises from the end of the curving street like a red sandstone crown thrust toward heaven, an offering to the One in whose honor the abbey was built. We'll take a proper tour of it tomorrow, but shall we stop now, just for a moment?

A dozen vehicles are scattered around the car park, unattended. At the abbey gate stands a young couple wearing frayed blue jeans and gazing upward. We unfold ourselves from the front seats, stretch out the kinks in our legs, then claim a spot ten steps away, giving the couple some elbow-room.

Looking up, I can't keep from sighing. Though the wooden roof has been gone for centuries and the floor is carpeted with grass, enough of the lofty stonework remains to give us a sense of its former glory. Both tradition and Rev. Dick tell us of "maiden ladies who kept a ferry and displayed both their piety and their muscularity by transporting all the freestone required from the other side of the Nith."[2] The long section with the lovely archways and pillars is the nave, where lay brothers would have been welcome.

When I point out the monk's choir, the holiest part of the church, I notice the twosome moving closer.

"Been here before, eh?" The young man grins and drapes a tanned arm around his partner's shoulders.

"First time for us," she confesses, blushing a little. "We're on our honeymoon." Their accents sound Australian.

"Congratulations." I smile, noting his single gold earring and a gold-capped tooth; Johnny Depp is alive and well in Galloway. "Where else have you traveled?"

"All over, really." He waves his free hand as he talks. "Argyll, Skye, the Trossachs…lots o' places. That's our bike over there." He gestures toward a BMW motorcycle bulging with gear and coated with dried mud. They really *have* seen Scotland. "We'll be sleepin' on Criffel tonight."

I try not to look shocked. *On Criffel? In May?* Here at the base the temperature will drop to fifty degrees once the sun sets. The Lord knows how cold it might be at a higher elevation. And then there's the wind...

"Don't be worryin' about us," he says, pulling his bride closer. "We camped out on Ben Nevis. We'll manage Criffel."

I can hardly protest. Ben Nevis in Inverness-shire is the highest mountain in the British Isles and claims some of the worst weather. Constant clouds, constant rain, constant wind, sometimes at gale force. *Oo aye,* they can handle Criffel.

We part company, though it's hard to leave Sweetheart Abbey after such a short visit. We'll have a good tromp about the grounds tomorrow.

Back in our car, we continue along the main road, now headed southeast. Criffel hovers over New Abbey like a gray green thunderhead—not threatening, just so very *present.* A stone bridge leads us out of the village, crossing a small burn fed by Loch Kindar; the stream's fresh waters will soon mingle with the salty Solway Firth. Criffel's height becomes more apparent, rising from the flat meadows at its base. Stone dykes and hedgerows mark the boundaries of pastures where sheep graze.

The A710 rides up and down like a gentle roller coaster, taking us past the small settlement of Drumburn—a half-dozen houses in a row—to a rise overlooking Carse Bay, gleaming in the late afternoon sun. The water reflects the blue sky above it. Gray brown silt gathers along its shores in sleek folds. I roll down the windows to breathe in the sea-tinged air, imagining the Irish Sea to the west and England not far to the south.

Soon we've reached the wee village of Kirkbean, with an old-fashioned red phone box and hedgerows lining both sides of the road leading to the old kirk. The name Kirkbean has nothing to do with beans and everything to do with Saint Beathan, circa AD 750. And here's a long-awaited signpost: Cavens Country House Hotel. I do hope you'll like the place. I have fond memories of Cavens, having spent my first night in Scotland here.

A lovely wooded drive ushers us in. I'll be glad to get out of this car, won't you? When I booked the room, I opted for the dinner package, so we won't have to venture out once we've settled in for the evening. But really, who would want to when you're staying in an eighteenth-century country house surrounded by six acres of gardens?

ROOM WITH A VIEW

Whitewashed exterior walls and windows everywhere, trimmed in gray, just as I remembered. The extensive grounds slope away from the house, providing a fine vantage point from every window. Keenly watched by its master, a dog romps about on the lawn. Not a breed I recognize: medium size, brown coat, black nose and ears, friendly. Dogs are welcome for a mere ten pounds per stay, though perhaps this one lives at Cavens free of charge.

I've seldom stayed in a British hotel or B&B—bed-and-breakfast—that didn't have a dog or two on the premises.

"Hullo!" An efficient-looking young woman in a navy-blue suit descends the front steps. "We have you booked in for two nights," she tells us. With only seven rooms to let, I imagine it's easier to keep track of guests. Both suitcases in hand, she guides us through the celery-colored entrance. "You're the only Americans with us just now."

"We'll try to behave," I assure her, at which she smiles. In all my trips to Galloway, I've seldom crossed paths with other American tourists; elsewhere in Scotland, but not this corner. Even Gallovidians stare at me, clearly dumbfounded. "You could go anywhere in the world, and you keep coming *here*?" I understand their confusion; growing up amid the Amish farmlands of Lancaster County, I couldn't fathom why tourists flocked to our area in the summer when they could have gone to the New Jersey shore.

Walking through the reception area, we're greeted by the scent of fresh lilies, arranged in a tall vase, and a glimpse of a large public room ahead. An interior designer would use words like *tasteful* and *understated* to describe the hotel's collection of comfy, upholstered furniture and gilt-framed oil paintings. Murmuring apologies for our heavy bags, we follow the housekeeper down one corridor, then another, before climbing a fine old staircase with two landings.

We've a nice room for our first night. "Kindar"—named for the loch on Criffel's northeastern slope—features antique twin rattan beds with tartan bedcovers in muted spring colors of peach, green, and yellow; a sunlit sitting room full of books; and a splendid view of the garden, which in the U.K. simply means the property adjoining a house, not necessarily flower beds and formal plantings. Still, lovely to look at and beautifully maintained.

Our helpful lass parks our luggage at the ends of the beds, not the least bit winded. "You are aware this room has only a shower, aye? No bathtub."

"No problem," I assure her, remembering my first visit years ago, when my husband and I stayed in a room at Cavens with a bathtub but no shower. The long, narrow, deep tub, typical to the U.K., was not built for my abundant American body. Just climbing in and out was an aerobic activity. I easily displaced five gallons of water, mostly because I couldn't stop laughing.

"Dinner at 7:00, then?" she says, looking about to see if all is in place. She deposits our room key on a pretty dressing table with an oval mirror, lots of little drawers, and a tapestry-shaded candlestick lamp, then departs with a nod, her duties well discharged.

We've time for a shower and a nap before dinner, in whatever order suits you. I'm off to see if the shower is any roomier than the tub.

IN A FOG

Last day my mind was in a bog…
A creeping cauld prosaic fog.

ROBERT BURNS

*M*y portable alarm clock on the bedside table is ticking rather too loudly. I stare at the numbers: *5:10? Is that a.m. or p.m.?* With the drapes pulled tight and my glasses over on the dressing table, I squint across the room, trying to guess. It feels like midnight. Or Wednesday.

I sit up, pulling the covers over my shoulders, thinking of those poor newlyweds huddled inside a thermal sleeping bag on Criffel. Our room is chilly, but at least a stiff breeze isn't blowing across our beds.

Yawning, I sort things out in my mind. We arrived at Cavens late Sunday afternoon, showered, napped, enjoyed a fine dinner of Galloway lamb and monkfish, walked around the gardens, then headed back to our room. The sun was still lingering over the horizon when we drew the curtains closed and crawled into our beds. So it has to be Monday morning.

Unless it's Tuesday morning.

Haar Haar

Och. I toss back the bedcovers, glad for my warm cotton pajamas and the socks on my feet. Parting the drapes, I'm greeted not by our bonny garden view but by a fog so dense you could tell me we were aboard a ship bound for America, and I'd believe you. It's not a *haar,* though; that cold, misty sea fog, which rolls in and refuses to roll back out, is a winter phenomenon. One December a friend and I drove along the Solway coast in such weather, which persisted all through the day, smothering land and sea in a chilly, dank shroud.

"'Tis a haar," one shopkeeper proudly told us, "an' thick as she comes."

We crawled along the A710 that day, stopping several times—at a grocer's, a pottery shop, a tearoom—if only to remind ourselves we were not the last people on earth, so strange was the sensation of seeing nothing but fog, hour upon hour.

I loved it, of course. So atmospheric.

Because we're on an island, the fog can disappear rather dramatically. One autumn morning I was headed west on the A708, a fine ribbon of road that winds through some wild country before reaching civilized Moffat. Fed by the waters of Saint Mary's Loch, fog blanketed the hills and crept across the road. Yet behind the fog shimmered the morning sun, waiting its turn.

All at once the fog was gone, as if *hoovered*—vacuumed, that is—by an unseen hand. I discovered all I'd been missing: children hopping from one foot to the other to keep warm at the bus stop; a stoop-backed man being walked by his sheep dog; teens riding their bicycles precipitously close to the road. How unnerving to realize they were there all along.

This morning's springtime fog will no doubt lift before we've finished our breakfast. Since they're not serving for another three hours, I plan to raid our sitting-room bookshelves and try to forget it's only midnight back home.

Besides, foggy mornings are ideal for crawling back under the covers with a borrowed novel.

FULL SCOTTISH BREAKFAST

Mist still swirls about the lawn at 8:00, but the warm yellow walls of the dining room add a bit of sunshine. Like most Scottish inns, Cavens has a lived-in feel, which only adds to its appeal. Not everything matches; Laura Ashley is not spoken here. The furniture has been lovingly collected over decades instead of purchased wholesale from a catalog. History hangs in the air like dust motes, not always visible but always present. Sir Richard Oswald, an influential Glasgow tobacco baron, married later in life and built Cavens for his bride. Two and a half centuries later we're enjoying the same gracious surroundings. Extraordinary when you think about it.

Some things do change over the years; the names of the lodging rooms, for one. Last time I was thrilled to discover a Crawford room at Cavens. Were the Oswalds and the Crawfords related? Might the original owners be long-lost ancestors on my mother's side?

When I asked about the Crawford connection, our host chuckled. "We had a ninety-five-year-old neighbor named Crawford and did it just to please her."

Oh.

Seated next to the bay window, an older couple sip their tea, looking out at the garden in companionable silence, while we patiently await our Full Scottish Breakfast, a phrase on the menu of every lodging place in Scotland, from five-star hotels to one-star hovels. It's a particular selection of foods with few variations: no french toast, no waffles, no bagels, no Danish pastries. Breakfast in this country is more substantial, meant to stoke your engines for a day of walking o'er the *braes*.

First, there's steaming hot porridge, if you like, or cold cereals with whole milk, and a dish of neatly chopped fresh fruit. Toast is next—white and wheat—cut diagonally, then slipped into a little metal rack to keep it crisp. I purchased such an item on my first trip, pledging never to serve toast any other way. Though it traveled home with me, I fear my toast rack has not surfaced in my kitchen since.

Galloway is known for its dairy farms, so you can count on real butter—not little pats on paper squares but an enormous slab on a china plate. A pot of thick-cut orange marmalade is on the table along with creamy organic honey, often flavored by heather or wildflowers. Unlike our clear, amber-colored honey back home, the Scottish version is more dense and less sticky, which makes it far easier to spread.

"Your hot breakfast, ladies." Two large plates land in front of us, served by our affable host, dressed in a rumpled blue sweater and trousers, a white apron tied around his waist. Hard-working folk, these Scots. His close-set eyes are kind and his smile, genuine. "Will you be needing anything else?"

I stifle a laugh. *Anything else?* Freshly pressed orange juice, one poached egg, a monstrous pile of sautéed mushrooms, half a tomato broiled with cheese, two rashers of bacon, which look and taste like ham—or better still, like Canadian bacon—plus two stout but watery link sausages called *bangers.* And more toast. And more tea.

"This should do it," I assure him, grateful he didn't automatically add black pudding to our plates, as some places do. I'll not spoil your appetite by describing the contents. If I said hog's blood was involved, would that be enough? Even if you didn't know the ingredients, the murky color, grainy texture, and earthy flavor might be enough to put you off your feed.

And we can't have *that,* not with a Full Scottish Breakfast before you and misty Galloway waiting to be explored.

HOLY GROUND

Blest be the hour she cool'd in her linnens,
And blythe be the bird that sings on her grave!

ROBERT BURNS

*J*udging by the grimace on your face, I'd say tiptoeing around the cemetery of the Kirkbean Parish Church after breakfast is not your idea of a good time. We'll not tarry long, just until the last of the fog dissipates and the museums open their doors.

The grass is soft underfoot—spongy and wet with dew—and shockingly green, as if a caretaker had spray-painted the grounds while we slept. It's also cooler than I expected. Though there's no breeze this morning, the air is dense with moisture, seeping through my cotton sweater. If I shiver occasionally, it's not because of our present location.

Odd, isn't it, how we whisper in kirkyards? Respect for the dead, perhaps; a desire to maintain the utter stillness of the place; and a certain awareness of our mortality, knowing our own names will be chiseled in stone someday. When my turn comes, I may borrow an epitaph from a 1730 gravestone in nearby Annan Parish: "Beneath this stone in silent slumber sleeps / Her sacred dust, whose soul sweet Jesus keeps."[1] Such tender, comforting words.

Like many Church of Scotland preaching houses, Kirkbean was built along austere lines, with clear glass windows, a central bell tower, and no ornamentation. Gray harled walls and plain, white trim give the church a dour look any minister of old would approve, yet the wooden front doors are painted a stunning peacock blue.

Not long after the church was erected in 1776, its minister deemed the structure "elegant, convenient, and sufficient."[2] William Craik of Arbigland—an estate little more than a mile from here—is said to have designed the building. Tuck that name where you can find it; more on Mr. Craik before our trip ends.

NAMING NAMES

Aren't the headstones *huge*? Five and six feet tall—many of them facing east, anticipating the Lord's return—with artwork and epitaphs carved on both sides. Character names for my novels are what I'm after this morning, combining a first name from one stone and a surname from another.

In Kirkcudbright, I once found several keepers: Ivy Gray, Basil Cairns, and John Cruick Shanks Alexander. Sounds like a cast list from a late-thirties British film. Farther north in Luss I jotted down Gilbert Mac-Brayne, Duncan McGilchrist, and Alison Eliza Wilson. Wonderfully chewy names and decidedly Scottish. And when we worship in Minnigaff next Sunday, you'll see the old kirkyard that yielded Isabella Ann Callender, Alexander MacLelland, and Elizabeth McQueen Broadfoot. That last one is especially regal, as if one should curtsy when saying it.

Most Lowland names sound far more common. Here's a George Martin and a Mary Scott, though mixing and matching these two might bring to mind a crusty general and a flying Pan. (If you're under thirty, that would be George C. Scott in *Patton* and Mary Martin in *Peter Pan*.) But isn't this name interesting? Captain Nichol Whitehead, born in 1787. A ship's captain, one can only presume, since he lived in Carsethorn—

"Good mornin'!"

Startled, we turn to find a woman padding across the thick carpet of grass, lifting her feet as if fearful of dinting the sod. Perhaps sixty years old, with streaks of gray in her light brown hair, she's shorter than many of the gravestones and wearing a plastic parka.

Holding up a bucket of water, she announces, "I'm here to see about my great-great-grandmother."

Instinctively, we step back to make room for her. We're strangers among the departed; she's family. But the bucket puzzles me. Perhaps if it had flowers in it…

From her trouser pocket she pulls a toothbrush and swishes it around in the water, then closes in on a marble monument, all business. "A foggy morning after a rainy night is best. Softens the moss." She chooses an inscription at shoulder height and begins to scrub in a circular motion. "My family's from Carsethorn, but I live in New Abbey now."

She'd not moved far. Carsethorn is a mile east of here: a sleepy bay-side village that once served as the port for Dumfries, trading goods and passengers with the Colonies through much of the eighteenth century.

We watch in fascination as the moss slowly gives way beneath the soft bristles. I can't stop myself from asking, "Would a wire brush help? Or some bleach?"

Her hand stills, and she frowns over her shoulder. "Either one would irreparably damage the stone. Water is what's called for." She pulls a sponge from her bucket and gently rubs it across the chiseled inscription. "Patience helps as well."

I glance at my watch and realize *your* patience has probably run its course. Enough of kirkyards. "We'll be off then."

She keeps scrubbing. "You weren't planning on visiting the John Paul Jones cottage, were you?"

That is precisely where we're headed.

"Closed on Mondays," she informs us. "Except bank holidays, and that's in a fortnight."

Though "bank holiday" sounds like a riotous party held at a financial institution, in truth, banks and other businesses close their doors on a

curious collection of Mondays, giving residents a three-day weekend—
apparently so they can visit the John Paul Jones cottage in Kirkbean.

"Perhaps tomorrow—"

"Aye," she agrees, frowning at a stubborn clump of moss, "Tuesday's
the ticket."

We murmur our thanks and leave her to her sponging and brushing.
Now that the fog has lifted as far as Criffel's heights, our short drive north
to New Abbey will be far more scenic.

Not a car on the road, not a soul in sight. Just undulating macadam,
named for John McAdam, a Scottish civil engineer who devised an inexpensive method of building roads from crushed stones and gravel in the
1790s. On either side of us the pastures are greener than ever, thanks to last
night's rain. The estuary at low tide resembles mercury in a thermometer:
thick and silvery, in no hurry to rise. Wildflowers are scattered across the
meadows: tiny yellow flowerets and white-topped clover.

I scan the rutted track leading up to Ardwall Mains, the likely route
our motorcycling honeymooners took last evening. My maternal instincts are roused: Did they manage to stay warm? Do they both have
colds now?

Maybe they wisely rolled out their sleeping bags at Ardwall, well
below the summit, and took in the view of Loch Kindar and its two wee
islands—one natural, one artificial. The larger one, with a submerged
causeway leading to the shore, is the site of a church even older than the
abbey. And the smaller islet is a man-made *crannog*. Built of stones resting
on piles of oak driven into the loch bed, the ancient lake dwelling provided a watery means of defense and easy fishing.

How ancient, you ask? Think Bronze Age. Or Iron Age.

Just don't think of old age. Next to a crannog, we're younger than springtime.

Mr. Holland's Ewer

We're barely over the bridge into the village when I guide our car down a lane that leads to the New Abbey Parish Church. Edging both sides are stone dykes and abundant shrubbery adorned with pink blossoms. The church, nestled within this wooded setting, is a mid-Victorian beauty, built of gray granite and dressed in red sandstone with a tall, slender belfry and a many-peaked roof.

I worshiped here one Sabbath in May when Rev. William Holland was in the pulpit. A cherub face with hardly a wrinkle, a fringe of silver hair, a kind demeanor, a wise soul—that's Bill Holland. After the service, I approached him at the door and introduced myself. "I wonder if you know any of this parish's history?"

He flashed me a canny smile. "Come to the manse for tea."

I've been going to the manse for tea ever since. The minister's house, situated next to Sweetheart Abbey, is two centuries old and encircled with a stone dyke topped by a close-clipped hedgerow that wraps up and over the gate. But it's the couple who live there—two of the dearest people on God's green earth—that make the manse so special.

Bill's wife, Helen, is a spry bundle of energy. No sooner does she settle down on the carpeted floor with her tea than she's popping up to fetch a fresh supply of shortbread or to locate a book for Bill or to show me her hand-knitted sweaters in a Fair Isle pattern.

Bill and Helen share my fascination with history. On one occasion he disappeared up the stair and returned with a pewter ewer in his hands and a twinkle in his eye. "I thought you'd want to have a look at this."

The tall pitcher, polished to a burnished sheen, had an ageless beauty with its simple lines, round lid, and graceful handle.

"It's for pouring the communion wine," he explained, showing me the date inscribed on the pewter: 1759. The year Handel died and Burns was born.

As I cradled history in my hands, Bill described the serious nature of New Abbey's twice-a-year sacrament. "In those days, elders would visit each parishioner. Those who were spiritually and morally worthy received a communion token to be presented to the minister before they partook of the elements." On museum jaunts I've seen such tokens—square, circular, or oblong, made of tin, brass, pewter, or lead, and no bigger than a coin.

Bill described the communion season of old. "Folk would fast on Thursday, have a service of preparation on Saturday, receive communion on the Sabbath, then have a thanksgiving service on Monday."

This morning as you and I stroll about the peaceful church grounds, I remember Bill's words and think of my typical communion experience: a brief time of prayer, an even briefer time with the elements. Could I willingly forgo meals to prepare my body for the Lord's Supper? Would I gladly invest so many days in celebrating his gift of mercy? Though I do acknowledge God's grace every hour of every day, the old ways of worship call to me like a distant echo.

Wait. Rest. Meditate. Listen.

GILDED ARCHES

The arches striding o'er the new-born stream,
The village glittering in the noontide beam.

ROBERT BURNS

After wending our way north through New Abbey, we cross
the bridge and are swallowed up by the lofty pines. I blink,
letting my eyes adjust as I move my foot to the brake pedal; the entrance
to Shambellie House Museum of Costume is easy to miss along the deeply
shaded road.

Here we are: gates on the left and an empty car park surrounded by
woods. The steady ascent on foot is longer than I remembered. As elsewhere in Scotland, right about the time you'd like to sit down, a bench
appears. They're invariably wet, but one can't have everything.

Shambellie's leafy drive is lined with rhododendrons and hydrangeas, and the garden contains a surprising variety of trees. At last we enter a clearing where a baronial mansion commands the scene from a raised bank. The gray stone Victorian was built to be admired: a turret, a bay window with a parapet, a round stair tower with a cone-shaped roof, and crowstepped gables.

Having paid our three pounds, we step inside the hall, admiring the grandfather clock and a portrait of William Stewart, father of the man who built Shambellie House. Since he too was named William Stewart, was he called "Junior"? "Willie"? Actually, this Stewart line produced so many Williams he might well have been called "Bill XVI."

It's a pleasure to be in a house that's not been "remuddled." The dark woodwork, the broad staircase, the mantelpieces—all are true to the era. But it's the carefully dressed mannequins visitors pay their pounds to see.

Each room re-creates a different time period. The dining room takes us to the summer of 1895, where the scene is set for an elegant dinner party and bejeweled women are appropriately attired in gowns stitched from black lace, claret velvet, and gold satin damask. Up the stair, we find a bathroom depicting a chilly November morning in 1905—very Spartan, with its wainscoted blue walls and white bath fixtures—and a sitting room as it might have looked in the summer of 1882, with four figures in cotton gowns and bustles. Other rooms feature more recent furnishings and attire—a drawing room reproducing 1945, a library circa 1952—but it's the older ones that interest me most.

I'm itching to pull out my camera, but photography is not permitted. When we reach the gift shop, I'm dismayed to find no guidebook detailing the clothing and furnishings. Couldn't someone have captured these lovely period rooms on film?

The doe-eyed young woman behind the cash register is sympathetic. "Aye, 'tis a shame. We've only a photocopied list of the costumes, which our guides use."

When she pulls out a dog-eared sheaf of papers from underneath the counter, my heart flutters. *Details.* Writers crave details. "Might I…take a look?" She willingly hands over the stapled pages, and I quickly flip through them, talking breathlessly into my tape recorder. "Dolman coat…silk poplin…guipure lace…"

"Tell you what." The cashier's voice is low, conspiratorial, as she leans over the counter, her curly black hair smelling faintly herbal. "You can keep it. That's an old copy, and—"

"Bless you!" The papers are already folded and jammed in my purse. "I'll put it to good use and think of you warmly when I do."

She blushes at my American effusiveness, then rings up our purchases: a book on Paisley shawls and another on laundry bygones. After her kindness, I felt obligated to buy *something*.

Stepping outside, we discover the day has brightened noticeably. Shall we take a tour through the corn mill? By *corn* they mean any grain, oats in particular; American-style corn on the cob is called *maize* or *sweet corn* here.

I've enjoyed the historic site's video— *The Miller's Tale*— twice before. One odd fact sticks in my mind: in the eighteenth century, people were so afraid to immerse themselves in water and thereby risk illness that they typically bathed *once a year*. (Historical novelists are known to overlook a few distasteful realities when telling their tales; I chose that one.)

The corn mill is nicely restored and highly photogenic with its whitewashed exterior and a blue and red painted cart parked beside a display of finishing stones, used to process the meal. A short walk around the property gives us a look at the mill *lade* and the huge wooden waterwheel. Farther afield we spot the placid millpond lined with granite from Criffel. Aren't the houses along this winding road worth the climb? Quite old indeed—seventeenth century—with rubble walls and tiny windows.

As we continue uphill, our senses are assaulted with greenery: sweet-scented bushes and close-cropped hedgerows, colorful walled gardens and tall, leafy trees—all surrounded by a plush carpet of grass fairly begging for a picnic. The birdsong is lovely, sweet and melodic, and the abbey serves as an exquisite bookend on the far side of the village—that is to say, not far at all.

A SECOND LOOK

Sweetheart Abbey yields a love story well suited to the Middle Ages. Lady Devorgilla, a thirteenth-century noblewoman, honored her late husband, John Balliol, by carrying about his embalmed heart in a silver-and-ivory casket. (If she'd carried around his hand or his foot, we might find the whole thing less appealing.) For two decades Lady Devorgilla kept his heart close to hers, until the day she was laid to rest within the walls of the abbey founded in his memory, giving the abbey its lovely name, *Dulce Cor,* or Sweet Heart.

Preservation of the abbey now falls to Historic Scotland, a government agency that safeguards the country's historical structures. I'm a card-carrying member, happy to pay my annual dues whether I travel abroad or not. For you, the Explorer Pass we picked up at the corn mill is a good value for our ten-day visit.

With a light breeze ruffling our sleeves, we enter the open cloister area through a freestanding arched doorway, the rosy red sandstone warmed by the midday sun. Shields bearing the Douglas insignia—a heart and three stars—are emblazoned over our heads. Galloway is thick with Douglas lore, beginning with William Douglas, one of Sir William Wallace's stalwart supporters in the fight for independence from England. Every kirkyard in the region features a Douglas grave, it seems, and more than one Lowland castle housed the powerful family. Various Douglas men have been called "Good," "Grim," and "Gross," not to mention "Duke" and "Earl." We'll hear the name often this week.

Not every Historic Scotland property has a staff member on hand, but this one does. See that wooden shack on the right? And emerging from it, a friendly-looking fellow to greet us. Striding across the grass—checked wool cap pulled low across his forehead, piercing blue eyes shining beneath the brim—the lanky older gentleman is a dead ringer for one of my characters. Has fictional Duncan Hastings, the overseer of Auchengray farm, come to life in modern Galloway?

"Ye'll be wantin' to have a look 'round." Even his rough voice sounds like Duncan's.

When we're quick to show him a membership card and newly minted pass, he tries not to smile. Obviously we fit our roles too: enthusiastic tourists.

He nods toward the abbey. "Not likely to have many visitors on a Monday. Would ye like me to walk ye *aboot*?" His musical "about" sounds familiar. Our Canadian neighbors pronounce the word quite the same way, and for good reason: many a Scot immigrated to Canada. We match his long-legged gait as he leads us toward a series of large, grassy rectangles bordered with rocky whinstone. After the Reformation, abbeys across Scotland were dismantled and the stones carted away by local farmers for building dykes, leaving much for our imaginations to fill in.

"This is the warming room." He points toward the remnant of a fireplace. "'Twas the only place in the monastery with heat, so the monks gathered here for a short time each day. And that's the parlor," he says, moving us closer to the nave. "The one place the monks were allowed to have informal conversations."

I imagine them standing about in their rough, woolen habits, nodding their tonsured heads at one another, speaking in lowered voices, trying to stay warm as the winter winds blew across Galloway.

We continue walking as our impromptu guide describes a typical day for a Cistercian monk—prayers, worship, prayers, reading, prayers, work, prayers—with little time for sleep, food, or leisure. "They were famous for their farming and horse-breeding skills."

"And their faith." I pause at the entrance to the south transept, where Lady Devorgilla's effigy is displayed, and gaze into the presbytery. Light streams through the roofless abbey, the pillars casting massive shadows. Where blue sky now outlines the stone tracery in the windows, stained glass once transformed beams of light into brilliant shafts of color.

I already own dozens of photos of Sweetheart Abbey; I take dozens more. Gothic arches with broad peaks direct the eye heavenward. The classic design is repeated over and over in windows and doorways too numerous to count. I see you snapping away and am glad to know the serene beauty of this place has captured your heart as well.

Since our Duncan has taken his leave, off to assist some new arrivals, perhaps it's time we moved on as well. Wouldn't a pot of Earl Grey be just the thing?

ROOM FOR TEA

Mere steps away from Sweetheart resides Abbey Cottage, my favorite tea-room in Dumfries and Galloway; The Smithy on the High Street in New Galloway is a close second. We can duck in the side door and follow the hallway into the tearoom itself or enter through the gingerbread-festooned front door and poke about the gift shop first.

Right, then. The gift shop.

Shelves filled with local preserves. Counted cross-stitch kits of local landmarks. Pewter, pottery, and beeswax candles. And silver jewelry, ever my weakness. Earrings make the best souvenirs: fun to wear and easy to pack.

Glass jars of lemon curd—a sweet, creamy spread made of eggs, sugar, and lemon juice—are a different story. Breakable, perishable, and messy indeed if crushed inside a suitcase, lemon curd is a risky choice. Even so, I always take home one jar, swathed in Bubble Wrap. Weeks from now, spreading lemon curd on my morning English muffin, I'll close my eyes and think of Scotland.

Morag McKie, the proprietress of Abbey Cottage, isn't in just now. A cheery young woman—perhaps one of her daughters—slips our purchases into a paper sack. "Will ye be joinin' us for lunch?"

Aye, lass, we will.

Seated in the adjoining tearoom, aglow with early afternoon sunshine, we study the menus. The *starters*—an ideal word for appetizers—include haggis. You game? Another time, perhaps. Jacket potatoes are served with your choice of fillings: savory tuna, smoked chicken, cottage cheese, or—trying again—haggis. Not yet? I fear my earlier description of toasties has made you wary; they're quite delicious here. I'm going for the salmon pâté and cream cheese sandwich.

Tea is served shortly after we place our orders. More than a simple cup of hot water with a bag, tea here involves two pots each and a whole trayful of useful items. With the Twinings label dangling from under the lid, my brewing Earl Grey is placed before me, then an extra pot of hot water. The first time I saw this, I thought, *Brilliant! Twice as much tea!* and lifted the lid on my pot to transfer the dripping bag to teapot number two, making rather a mess of things in the process.

The entire tearoom stared at me, aghast.

A willing student, I asked my waitress what one was supposed to do with the second pot.

"Just add a wee bit o' the plain water to yer tea when it gets too strong."

Move the water, then, not the bag.

Two small pitchers appear on our table—one with cream, one with milk—a bowl of tan and white sugar cubes, and two teacups on saucers. Best for last: a real teaspoon. Half the size of what Americans consider a teaspoon, this little beauty is perfect for scooping up a cube of sugar and stirring your hot drink. Because of its size, the spoon isn't easily knocked off the saucer or inadvertently launched across the table. (I've done both.)

Our lunch follows in good time; no one comes to New Abbey because they're in a hurry. Meanwhile, we take another sip of tea, admire the abbey, and contemplate the selection of sweets and home-baked goods. I'm having the fruit scone with jam and cream, hoping you'll join me. It too involves a host of miniature dishes and a certain ritual to fully appreciate this British treat.

ROMANCING THE SCONE

The scone (rhymes with "gone") should be sliced in half—tricky, I know, when they're so crumbly. Richer in flavor and denser in texture than an American biscuit, scones come in plain, *wholemeal,* cheese, or fruit varieties. I've yet to see Scottish scones with chocolate chips or cinnamon swirls; either flavor might interfere with what we're about to do.

Is it my imagination, or is our waitress tarrying by the door, watching us? Never mind. You're going to bowl her over with your scone-slathering ability.

First, a thin coat of butter. Next comes that little pot of raspberry jam. Do be generous with your spoon. Now for the clotted cream, light as any whipped cream yet with a different consistency and a far superior flavor. Spoon it on top, hiding all that lovely jam, so each bite is a surprise.

Do keep your napkin handy, because if you've done this right, you'll soon be wearing a spot of cream on the end of your nose.

Oh, do I have one there too?

The next several minutes are blissfully quiet—lots of sighing and smiling and napkin dabbing—before we plan the balance of our day. We'll drive along the coast to Southerness, home to one of the oldest lighthouses in Scotland, built in 1748. Then we'll take a walk along the Solway and see if we can spot any black-and-white oystercatchers with their bright orange beaks and noisy calls. After that, a bit of reading in the garden at Cavens, a nap if you like, and we'll dress for dinner.

Can tomorrow be our third day in Scotland? One moment it feels like we've been here three weeks, another three hours. After a good night's sleep, the morning will begin with our delayed visit to the John Paul Jones cottage, where history resides in humble surroundings and a certain rumor lingers.

HISTORY LESSON

The crafty Colonel leaves the tartan'd lines,
For other wars, where he a hero shines.

ROBERT BURNS

*T*he sky is cloudless and the sun bright, yet our sweaters are no match for the wind. "Ye'll be wanting proper coats," our host at Cavens warned us a bit ago when we settled our bill. Now I see why.

Yesterday's foggy dawn is only a memory. This morning the air is clear, brisk, and chilly, more like March than May. Our one-mile drive from Kirkbean was mostly uphill on a narrow track, taking us east past the gates of the Arbigland estate to the rocky cliffs overlooking the Solway Firth. We climb out of our car, toss our map into the backseat, already strewn

with guidebooks and brochures, and head toward our first adventure of
the day.

History is in the eye of the beholder, and much depends on the time
and place in which one is standing. Today John Paul Jones is heralded in
our homeland as the father of the United States Navy and a champion of
the Age of Sail. Teddy Roosevelt once decreed, "Every officer in our navy
should know by heart the deeds of John Paul Jones,"[1] and many would-
be heroes have quoted the naval captain's legendary declaration: "I have
not yet begun to fight!"

But in 1793, Rev. Edward Neilson had little good to say about the trai-
torous sea captain, born in Kirkbean Parish five decades earlier. John Paul
didn't add "Jones" to his name until he'd killed an insolent crewman in
Tobago and fled to America to reinvent himself, tossing aside his Scottish
allegiances.

The minister wrote, "Of this person's character, this parish cannot
boast." He cited several examples of John Paul's treachery, foremost "his
conduct to his native country during the American war" and other
"instances of ingratitude and want of patriotism…over which, for the
honour of humanity, we would wish to draw a veil."[2] Oh my.

Thirty years later another local author, John Mactaggart, wrote at
length on "Paul Jones, the Pirate," naming him "the late celebrated sea
robber; a Gallovidian, I am rather sorry to say, but he was a clever devil"
with "strong talents of the infernal stamp." Mactaggart described the sea-
man's "mad, ambitious, aspiring nature" and his "savage temper," making
no reference whatsoever to the pivotal role Jones played on behalf of
America's fledgling navy.[3]

So…Scottish bad boy or all-American hero? We walk along the gravel

path to the two-room cottage where John Paul was born, curious to see if time has softened the parish's ill opinion of their famous son.

Quite a view of the Solway we have from up here, its shimmering blue surface blending into the horizon. No wonder young John Paul dreamed of the sea while inhaling the salty air in his sleep. At the museum entrance, two flags proudly wave in the stiff breeze: the white-on-blue Saint Andrew's Cross, or saltire, and our own Stars and Stripes. Very diplomatic.

Once we duck inside the cottage, away from the wind, the cold is not so noticeable, though both of us are still shivering as we take in our surroundings. I try to picture a family of seven lodging in this humble dwelling. Two rooms are sparsely decorated and dimly lit by the smallest of windows. A hearth stands at each end, hemmed in by whitewashed rubble walls, with low ceilings above and uneven flagstone floors below. A stepladder leads to a sleeping loft for the children. The single, curtained box bed boasts a white and red quilt and a pristine dust ruffle, though I doubt the mistress could have kept it so clean.

John's mother was a skilled housekeeper, however, and worked for the esteemed William Craik of Arbigland. You'll recall his name from yesterday; he designed the Kirkbean Parish Church. The gardener for Craik's estate was John Paul Sr.—John's father, unless the unkind rumors whispered around Kirkbean of old were true.

"Ye'll be wanting to watch the video?" The museum's docent, a woman full of years, gestures toward an adjacent room with pale gray walls and a wooden floor—a replica of a ship cabin, built to scale. Soon we're immersed in a sea battle waged in September 1779 between the *Bonhomme Richard,* an American navy vessel captained by Jones, and the *Serapis,* a British man-of-war. Though the death toll was high, Jones emerged victorious.

"Most exciting," I comment to our hostess when the brief video ends and we prepare to take our leave. At the door I pause, wondering if I dare ask her to confirm or deny what at least two reliable sources have suggested: that the landowner, Mr. William Craik, and not John Paul Sr., was the true father of our swashbuckling naval captain. Such liaisons between *laird* and servant were not uncommon.

"It's come to my attention…" My words start to unravel. "That is, I've read that John Paul…" When the older woman cocks her ear, listening intently, I get cold feet, and not from the flagstone floor. "Is it true he, um, died in Paris when he was only forty-four?"

"Alone." She sighs as if wishing she'd been with her hero at the end.

With a murmur of thanks, we quit the cottage, tossing our unasked question to the Solway winds.

ON THE ROAD TO BEESWING

Bid New Abbey farewell, my friend; we're on to gardens and castles.

Passing the corn mill for the last time, we cross the bridge and bear left on a slender road marked "Beeswing—5 miles." The road is stick straight at first, lined with dense hedgerows and towering pine trees. Glenharvie, an old snuff mill converted to a fine two-story home in the early nineteenth century, soon appears on the left, framed by hills and surrounded by meadows. According to historic records, Glenharvie has a *doocot,* or dovecote, though the house sits too far back from the road for us to pick out the pyramid-shaped roof. Wouldn't it be grand to fall asleep to the cooing of doves in the garden?

We're beginning to climb now. A decrepit stone dyke edges the road, and clumps of bright yellow gorse—bushy evergreens with bright gold flowers—dot the fields. New Abbey Pow flows through the narrow valley, its steep banks hiding the slow-moving stream below. Rather wild country, this, with an untamed look.

> Cultivated fields gave way to more rugged land, with gnarled old trees and outcroppings of rocks the size of cows. Past the dark fell that rose to her left, the road straightened for the last mile home, much of it uphill.
>
> *Thorn in My Heart*

Continuing on our northwesterly route as the road curves and undulates, we pass Mossyard, a century-old row of one-story white cottages. Straight ahead is Lotus Hill—spelled *Lowtis* in the past. Little more than half the size of Criffel, the verdant mound still draws our attention. Thick-fleeced white sheep with black pigment on their faces, ears, and legs graze in the pastures. Amid them, a Highland *coo* makes an unexpected appearance: an enormous creature with a shaggy, orange red coat and sharp horns poking out at dangerous angles. Such cows are typically seen farther north, not in a Lowland pasture. I'll slow down so you can snap a photo.

And here is Auchengray on our right, birthplace of the fictional McBride sisters. A stone dyke leads to a whitewashed farmhouse and steading. The land, recently cleared of conifers, is littered with rocks. A bit northeast of the house is Auchengray Hill—always bigger than I remember—with sheep crowding the adjoining pasture. Though I don't know the family who resides at Auchengray, I wave in passing, grateful to have spent many imaginary months on their farm.

In less than a mile we come upon Glensone, located on the glen's sunny side, as the name suggests. Perhaps the nicest property on this road, Glensone features several buildings neatly cobbled together, a pretty garden, and a clay tennis court. The skinny road running beside it climbs straight up Troston Hill, cutting through some of the roughest, rockiest farm and forestry land I've seen in Galloway.

We're nearing the five-mile mark when a lovely stretch of water appears, framed by a series of gentle hills on the far shore: Loch Arthur, as in King Arthur. Some enthusiasts claim Arthur's legendary Excalibur rests at the bottom of this loch, though no trace of it has been found. What *has* been located beneath Loch Arthur's tranquil surface is yet another ancient crannog. For my novels I used the eighteenth-century name of Lochend so as not to muddy the waters with Arthurian legend, but it does add to the romance of the setting.

And now we've reached Beeswing, a wee village that also bore the name Lochend until the mid-nineteenth century, when a new owner purchased Lochend Inn and renamed the place Beeswing in honor of the winning racehorse that provided the capital. (Makes perfect sense to this Kentucky woman, who drives on Man o' War Boulevard.)

MAXWELL HOUSE

After the tree-lined loch, the countryside feels wide open now, a vast expanse of sky, farmlands, and distant hills. As our quiet lane intersects the busy A711, we wait for the row of cars flying past, then cross the main road and continue west, farm names serving as our landmarks: left at Killywhan, on past Old Blairshinnoch. And here's Drumcoltran Tower, a sixteenth-century castle once owned by a Lord Maxwell, squeezed between farm buildings and a handsome old house. The oblong tower looms three stories tall yet boasts only a half-dozen windows facing the road.

Despite the car park and a Historic Scotland sign, I still feel like we're intruding; Drumcoltran is a working farm. If we stick to the marked path, we'll avoid the worst of the mud beneath these old trees. As we pass a gaggle of honking geese, I'm grateful for the cool breeze that lessens the pungent aroma of livestock.

The entrance is around the corner, and high above it, a stone panel inscribed in Latin: *Cela secreta,* or "Conceal secrets." The other Latin injunctions are equally forthright: "Speak little. Be truthful. Remember death." A solemn charge to family members, do you suppose, or cautionary words for Lord Maxwell's guests circa 1570?

Inside on the ground floor we find a vaulted cellar with arched walls and windowsills deeper than a yardstick. The air is dank and musty, and the sound of bleating calves, muted. We have to imagine the wooden crossbeams, long lost to decay, which would have formed the bedchamber floor above us. I see Lady Maxwell had a garderobe—a privy, if you like. In the corner is a narrow, circular stair. The stout rope hanging down serves as a makeshift railing for brave souls who want a better look at the upper floors.

The sharp bark of a dog makes us both jump, then glance toward the doorway. More visitors, by the sound of it; a cue for our departure. En route to the car we pass a middle-aged couple; all nod at one another and smile a little. Before long we've tooled through the village of Kirkgunzeon (turn the *z* into a *y*, and you'll say it perfectly) and are back at the A711, which we take southwest toward Dalbeattie.

Our hilly road curves and dips as farm names catch our eye; Lower Porterbelly, Meikle Culloch, and then a chillingly familiar one for my readers: Edingham Farm, home to those dastardly (albeit fictional) Douglas brothers.

We carry on through the town of Dalbeattie—like Aberdeen, it's known for its granite quarries—only to be stopped on the one-lane Buittle Bridge, waiting for the traffic light to change. There's your first look at Urr Water, running headlong toward the Solway.

Less than five hilly miles over the A745 and we'll enter one of the busiest burghs in Galloway, once no more than a scattering of cottages known as Causewayend, then as Carlinwark, until Sir William Douglas purchased the land in 1791 and laid out a Georgian town bearing his family name.

BURGH OF BARONY

Ye yet may follow where a Douglas leads!

ROBERT BURNS

*U*nlike Dumfries, which grew over centuries, Castle Douglas was a planned town, carefully laid out on a grid with parallel streets—Queen, King, and Cotton—and equidistant cross streets. With Sir William as landowner, Castle Douglas was deemed a burgh of barony and permitted to hold weekly markets. As you'll soon see, shopping is still the thing to do in Castle Douglas, a market town with nearly four thousand residents and one notable castle.

We enter from the northeast along the busy auction mart and are soon faced with a traffic circle that offers more options than most foreign drivers want. But aren't the flowers planted around it lovely? Besides, we can drive around the circle until we figure out which way is best.

Since Queen Street is more residential than commercial, meaning fewer pedestrians and more parking, we'll head that direction after we take a side trip up Market Street and find the public library. Not to check out books, mind you; we won't even go inside. I just want you to see the place. Isn't she a red sandstone beauty? More than a century old, with a round tower built into the crook of its L-shaped design. But it's the tree in the front garden that makes getting out of our car worthwhile.

The scientific name, *Araucaria araucana,* sounds like an incantation Harry Potter might use in a desperate moment. Most people call it a monkey puzzle tree, a name born when an Englishman in the nineteenth century commented that the tree would be a puzzle for a monkey to climb, so sharp edged are its thick and succulent leaves, clustered like an elongated pine cone into stiff branches.

Prehistoric looking, isn't it? Like a tree full of green snakes. Monkey puzzles arrived in Britain in 1795 when a fellow having dinner with the

governor of Chile pocketed a few of the tasty seeds, then sowed them on board ship. They grow well in the western districts of Scotland—I saw a gargantuan specimen in an Argyll garden—and the trees can live for centuries. You'd have to be a patient gardener to grow one, since seedlings take five to ten years before they even peep above the grass.

QUEEN AND KING

We drive several blocks farther down Queen Street until we spy an opening along the curb. No need to consult our watches: a church bell tolls the hour of eleven. Strolling down King Street, we pause in front of the Douglas Arms Hotel, a late-eighteenth-century coaching inn with a stark, white exterior and dark green trim. An 1827 sign lists the distances to prominent places—Edinburgh, 90; Glasgow, 92—making us feel very much in the center of things as we start up the other side of King Street.

Even on a weekday, we find a steady flow of shoppers popping in and out of doors or darting between cars. Rev. Dick called Castle Douglas a "delightful, modern town" with "well-appointed hotels, good shops, and busy population," creating "an air of mingled dignity and liveliness."[1] That's still true ninety years later as local folk, with the *Galloway News* tucked under an arm or a sack of vegetables in hand, sing out to one another.

"Mornin', Geordie!" one crusty gentleman calls across a line of cars waiting for the traffic light to change. His friend touches the brim of his cap and smiles, even as he keeps a firm grip on the pipe clenched between his teeth.

Butchers, bakers, and candlestick makers can still be found in Castle Douglas, known for its traditional shops. Pausing in front of a bakery, we try not to press our noses to the glass as we eye a rectangular steak pie, its thick crust oozing with a rich-looking gravy, and smaller ham-and-egg pies, round and deep. Sausage rolls are folded-over affairs, wrapped in thin, flaky dough. Scotch pies are offered as well, and *brid-ies,* horseshoe-shaped pastries stuffed with steak and onions. If you were thinking "pies" meant apple, cherry, or lemon, those are called *tarts* here. See them on the top shelf? Berry tarts, next to the fruit scones and soft yeast butteries…

Dinna *fash* yerself, lass. I've a fine place in mind for lunch.

We wander in and out of an art gallery, an antique store, and a smart dress shop, then cross the street to get a closer look at a storefront with an intriguing sign: "Don Philpott, Daughter and Granddaughters: Specializing in Country Clothing and Footwear for Field Sports." We assess the merchandise—Quiltknit sweaters and Hunter Wellies and Hoggs mole-skins—feeling out of our element even as we applaud Mr. Philpott for passing the family business on to his female heirs.

If we needed more O.S. maps or contemporary books about Scotland, Barry Smart, Newsagent has the best stock in the Stewartry. A few shops are clearly aimed at tourists: the display windows full of tartan-clad Scottie dogs, thistle-covered tea cozies, and Walkers shortbread. However, the linen towel describing the "Creation of Scotland" is worth stopping to read.

The story goes that when God created Scotland, he was so proud of his handiwork, he brought in the archangel Gabriel to have a look at the land's splendid mountains and beautiful scenery. Offered a taste of Scotland's native whisky, Gabriel took an appreciative sip and deemed it excellent, though he worried that God had been too kind to the Scots. "Won't they be spoiled by all these blessings? Should there not be some drawback?" To which God smiled and said, "Wait until you see their neighbors."

TOOLING AROUND THE GARDEN

Back in our car, though not for long, we continue down Queen Street past Lochside Park and along Carlingwark Loch, a lovely sheet of water, gilded by the noontide sun, with swans gliding across the surface and ducks waddling along the grassy banks. When you've had your fill, turn and look at the Buchan, a small row of whitewashed cottages predating Sir William's planned town by two centuries. The one-story dwellings were no doubt thatched at one time; now they have proper slate roofs and landscaping.

Two quick lefts, and we reach our destination. Threave Gardens and Estate is a National Trust for Scotland property, so no need to dig out your Historic Scotland pass. NTS also does their best to preserve the country's historic sites.

Driving through the gate, I feel a sense of peace wash over me. I am not a gardener; both my thumbs are brown, if not gray. But my mother was a gardener of such skill that strangers knocked on our front door and begged to see her flower beds. My strongest memories of my mother are linked to her garden: paging through the Burpee seed catalog with her in February as she made her wish list; posing beside her for our family Easter photos against a bright yellow spray of forsythia; clutching a handful of fragrant white peonies she'd chosen for a Memorial Day bouquet; sitting on a cool patch of grass on summer mornings, keeping her company while she weeded.

Is it any wonder I created a heroine who loved gardening?

> Leana plunged her hands into the loamy soil of her garden and breathed in the fresh morning air. Purple spikes of betony delighted the eye, even in October, and French marigolds still shone like tiny suns against the dark green leaves.
>
> *Thorn in My Heart*

We'll not see those particular flowers in bloom just yet, but I can promise a colorful display in the woodland garden and a healthy lunch in the Terrace Restaurant.

I eye the books and gifts in the Visitor Centre, proud of myself for resisting the urge to shop, then flash my blue membership card before we set forth into the gardens, sweetly scented and neatly edged with grass. I think you'll find your ten-pound admission a bargain.

The rose garden is first—if only it were July!—yet amid the colorless shrubs, a late display of showy tulips in red, pink, and purple fills in nicely. Our broad path slopes down into the woodland garden, guiding us past enormous rhododendrons covered with bright pink and white blooms. Obviously the temperate climate, warmed by the Gulf Stream, and the high silt content of the soil make for happy plants. I'm snapping pictures like mad. Since I can't grow rhodys any taller than my shoulder, I must be content photographing specimens the size of our house (well, nearly).

SUNLIGHT AND SHADOW

There's ne'er a flower that blooms in May,

That's half so fair as thou art!

ROBERT BURNS

W hen we emerge back into the sunshine a half hour later, our eyes are dazzled by the huge bank of daffodils in eye-popping yellow. A signature flower for Threave, daffodils are planted by the hundreds to bloom from mid-March to mid-May—trumpets lifted up, petals splayed like the rays of the sun. We bask in their yellow glory for a moment, then head for the herbaceous beds. Though we're a tad early for the bearded irises, Threave always has something of interest blooming, even if you have to bend down to appreciate it. My mother spent most of her gardening hours in such a posture.

On a late summer visit to Scotland, I brought one of my sisters with

me, armed with *Gardens of Scotland,* an annual publication that provides information on hundreds of private gardens that are open to the public for a nominal fee between April and September. Some residents open their garden gates at specific times, others by appointment, and the funds raised go to charity. A brilliant scheme, no? Argyll indicated the most gardens participating, so to Argyll my sister and I went.

One dear woman invited us into her kitchen for tea and biscuits (perhaps because we'd traveled such a distance or because my sister is a real gardener and not merely a flower enthusiast, like me). At another house, the hostess served us freshly baked apple cake on her patio, where a nearby bird feeder provided ongoing entertainment. Before the week was out, we'd explored ten memorable gardens and gained about ten pounds.

Speaking of which, what say you to lunch here at the Terrace Restaurant? The cook uses seasonal vegetables and herbs from Threave's kitchen garden, and the menu features sandwiches and baked goods sufficient to fortify our strength for the last venture of the day: a fourteenth-century tower house with a grim history.

Walking Tour

Hard to believe this narrow dirt road will take us to Threave Castle, part of the vast Threave Estate that includes Threave House—a Victorian summer home—and Threave Island.

First we bump along a farm road signposted off a traffic circle on the A75. I had to drive around twice, having missed the unobtrusive notice on the first pass. The sun is still high in the sky, but clouds are moving in, crowding out the blue. Lord willing, we'll make it to the castle and back before any rain appears.

Directed to a small car park opposite Kelton Mains, we feel like interlopers, just as we did at Drumcoltran. A family lives and works here—that's their livestock in the steading, their laundry hanging on the line. Have they grown accustomed to strangers walking through their fields? To the west of the farmhouse, Historic Scotland signage cautions, "Visitors to Castle Must Keep to This Path." An arrow points down a hard-dirt footpath with unpainted wood fencing on both sides. Threave isn't even visible from here. Can this be right?

The unlocked gate swings open easily enough, then closes on its own with a simple ball-and-chain device; Colonial Williamsburg has them too. Green pastures and fields stretch in all directions. We start out looking over our shoulders, as if any minute the farmer's wife might come charging after us, rolling pin raised. But, no, the back door remains closed, the steading quiet.

Our path is utterly straight and level. A stone dyke replaces the wooden fence on one side, and still the trail leads on through yet another weighted gate. Did that guidebook say ten minutes? For a jogger maybe. We catch a fleeting glimpse of the River Dee but still no castle. Along one side of our path a lazy burn wends its way through the lush grass, and on the other side a profusion of white wildflowers stands in tight clusters on tall stems. Sweet cicely is a likely guess.

At last we see Threave in the distance, framed by two flowering crab apple trees near the shore. The pink and white flowerets do little to soften the castle's severe appearance, which Rev. Dick deems "a certain barbaric majesty."[1] An appropriate place for the third Earl of Douglas—known as Archibald the Grim for his fierce countenance in battle—to breathe his last.

> A massive square tower rose in the distance, gray and
> foreboding as the clouds themselves…embrasures for
> archers' bows piercing the tower walls like eyes nar-
> rowed into menacing slits.
>
> *Thorn in My Heart*

Five stories tall, Threave Castle stands on an island in the middle of the Dee. Good defense plan, eh? The river is slow moving but deep, a broad ribbon of blue gray. At the wooden jetty, a brass bell with a rope pull invites us to summon a boatman to ferry us across. I give it a tenta- tive jangle. When nothing happens, I ring harder, and a helpful-looking fellow comes out of a tiny shack on the island—the world's smallest gift shop perhaps?—and climbs into his white motorboat.

Slight of build with wheat-colored hair, our boatman is dressed in a blue sweater and trousers, his Historic Scotland badge prominently displayed. Is he fifty years old? Sixty? Hard to say. His small craft purrs across the water as he calls out, "*Walcome* to Threave! I'll have ye there in no time."

We exchange glances, then stare down at the small boat. A foursome would find it a tight fit. Will the vessel deposit us into the watery Dee with the first step?

"Nothin' to worry aboot." He smiles, his sunburned face crinkling, and holds out his hand; he's managed nervous tourists before. "Step right in."

Brave you, going first. I take a deep breath and follow your lead, relieved when we're all three seated and making our way across the water. Odd that no other visitors are on the island. Though I'd boasted we'd have Galloway to ourselves, I didn't mean *this* solitary a tour. Maybe the long walk is a deterrent, or the prospect of a boat ride. However remote and foreboding, Threave is a historic site not to be missed.

THE HOUSE THAT DOUGLAS BUILT

My gaze is fixed on the whinstone castle, which grows taller and more intimidating as we approach. One of the earliest and largest towers in Gal-

loway, Threave was built as a Douglas stronghold, a formidable challenge for his many foes.

"Take your time," our guide urges as we gingerly climb out, unnerved by the looming ruin. Some castles exude a romantic air, others a sense of the melancholy or a hint of mystery. Threave is ominous, unsettling.

Sheer size is one explanation; a violent family history, another. The Black Douglases, as they were called, intermarried often with the royal family of Scotland, amassing lands, titles, and power eclipsed only by the king. Neither the English nor their neighbors in Galloway trusted the Douglas clan.

We enter the tower house built of rubble—rough, unfinished rock, colorless except where lichen adds a yellowish cast. A curving staircase in the corner and an arched fireplace in the wall give us a clue what the shadow-filled keep must have looked like six centuries ago, when the walls were plastered and hung with tapestries.

After an hour of climbing about, investigating the remains of the kitchen and the storage basement, the prison and the reception hall, we circle the tower house once more, keeping an eye on the sky. Thick clouds have moved in, blocking the sun entirely.

"Ye'll not want to get caught here in a storm," our boatman advises, hands clasped behind his back as he studies the heavens. "The footpath turns to mud, and there's nowhere to take shelter. Would ye be ready to go back?"

"Aye!" we assure him in unison, starting toward the jetty, pretending not to hear a distant rumble of thunder.

After our brief trip across the Dee, we leap off the boat and bolt up the path, heads down, chitchat kept to a minimum. Maybe this is what the guidebook meant by the walk taking ten minutes. Almost sprinting by the time we reach the car, we're soon buckled in, windshield wipers on full tilt. Next up is the Douglas House B&B, where our accommodations will be anything but grim.

UNDER THE WEATHER

Yon murky cloud is foul with rain,
I see it driving o'er the plain.

ROBERT BURNS

reakfast is due momentarily, and our morning includes a trip
to a bookshop. Other than the chance of more rain, could a
day begin on a happier note?

While Cavens is an upscale country house hotel, Douglas House features the homeyness of a true B&B, with just four rooms and a common
dining table. From the moment our hostess—blond, effusive, and altogether fun—greeted us at the door last evening, we felt like we'd come
to visit a friend. Her amiable husband is very much a part of things and
in charge of cooking our breakfast.

Last night we checked off our choices on a printed list featuring the usual Full Scottish Breakfast options. Porridge, bacon, mushrooms, and tea will do for me; you're planning on eggs, sausage, and a whole rack of toast.

And didn't we sleep well? Our ground-floor room was a subtle floral bouquet—on the wallpaper, on the frilly bedcovers, on the drapes—and the cream and pink bathroom was so large it had two long windows and a wicker armchair. The best part? A heated towel rail. Ah, the luxury of warm terry cloth on a chilly May morning.

Seated across from us are John and Frances, a husband and wife in their early eighties: silver-haired, generously wrinkled, and as bright-eyed and quick-witted as any couple you'd care to meet. Though they hail from the Lake District of England, John's family has roots in Galloway, and so they've come north for a few days.

Every inch a gentlewoman, Frances is dressed in a tailored skirt and sweater with a lace-collared blouse. I suspect she has a pair of white gloves in her handbag. Her manners are impeccable; I've never seen toast buttered with more care. She asks polite questions—"Were the daffodils blooming at Threave Gardens? How was your Moroccan lamb at the Kings Arms last evening?"—listens attentively, and then responds, "Ohhh, isn't that looovely!" to almost everything.

By the time our breakfast arrives, this charming woman has repeated the phrase at least a half-dozen times. I hide my smile behind a slice of toast. Truly, dear Frances is looovely. Our weather, however, is not. According to Rev. Holland of New Abbey, local precipitation falls into one of these categories: downpour, rain, drizzle, or Scots mist—a fine spray of moisture mixed with fog and whatever else is hanging about the atmosphere.

What we're having at the moment is a downpour.

"Won't last much longer," John insists, lifting his teacup toward the window as if daring the storm to continue.

"Rain shouldn't slow us down a bit," I assure him. "We're bound for a bookshop."

Frances beams at us. "Ohhh, isn't that looovely!"

BACK ROADS

Of course, we *could* take the A75 north to Kirkpatrick Durham. A straighter route and faster.

But speed is not what our ten days in bonny Scotland are about. Who would choose a main road at fifty miles per hour when you can drive half that speed and see twice as much? We'll return later today on the A75, but first we've a bit of countryside to explore.

Following King Street straight through the burgh, we're soon fresh out of houses and into the countryside—yet another quality I love about Scotland. When you reach the edge of a village—even a sizable place like Castle Douglas—the next thing you see is sheep. Or cows. Or a fine expanse of green. Not 7-Elevens or petrol stations or palm readers or car dealerships or tanning salons.

We're heading northeast on the Old Military Road, which once stretched from the bridge of Sark near Gretna Green to Portpatrick on the west coast. Och, what a view! Even drenched in rain, the hills and farms possess a timeless beauty. The road carries us up and down and over a narrow pair of bridges where an old stone house, Brigend, has stood for a long time.

And here's a small village with a uniquely Scots name—Haugh of Urr—*haugh* meaning level ground on the banks of a river, which in this case is the Urr. We turn southeast onto the B794, then veer off on a narrow road that will take us to the Urr Parish Church, established in 1606. Here it is, coming up on the left, with its dignified square tower topped by a pointed spire. As we saw at Durisdeer and Kirkbean, the gravestones march around the church, facing the same direction; in this case, parallel with the front door.

Of course, this isn't the original building. It was rebuilt from existing materials in 1750. When more space was required, the church was rebuilt again in 1815 for a total cost of one thousand pounds—no small sum then. More improvements came along, including a pipe organ and a stained-glass window, before the present church was erected in 1915. The parish held its quadricentennial celebration in 2006 with a flower festival, a fair on the grassy *glebe* adjoining the church, a harp evening, and a special service with three of the twenty ministers who've served this parish over the last four hundred years. A breathtaking number, isn't it?

The rain has stopped, just as John said it would. Could I coax you to join me in the kirkyard? Rather stay in the car?

Ah well, dearie. I'll not be long.

GRAVE THOUGHTS

The air is so moist I can feel my hair curling. When my feet sink into the spongy grass, I realize *you* made the wiser choice. Still, my curiosity longs to be assuaged. To whom does the large, roofless mausoleum belong?

Just as I suspected: the Herries of Spottes Hall, one of the oldest families in Urr Parish. Michael Herries buried his beloved wife here, as the stone marker to the left of the mausoleum gate indicates. The woman with her toothbrush and bucket must have stopped by; the inscription carved in sandstone is scrubbed clean.

> Here lies what was mortal of Anne Herries, spouse of
> Michael Herries of Spottes. A dutiful wife, an affec-
> tionate mother, and a sincere friend to all the virtuous
> part of mankind. As a memorial of her endearing
> worth and of his own tender recollection of her virtues,
> this monument is erected by her disconsolate husband
> July 1793.

Touching and beautifully worded. Bill has assured me that, if I die first, my gravestone will simply read: "She finally stopped talking."

The iron mausoleum gate allows a peek inside, where there's nothing but grass and gravel and a much more recent gravestone, listing several members of the family who've died over the past fifty years.

A drop of rain signals the end of my brief cemetery visit. Hurrying back to the car, I admire the line of Irish yews marking the boundaries of the church property and remember my last drive through this area on a brisk autumn day. An elderly woman was standing near the open church gate, so I pulled over to ask a question only a historical novelist would care about. "Ma'am, how old might these yews be?"

"Very, very old," she said emphatically.

"Do you imagine they were here in 1790?"

A frown creased her brow as if I'd suggested *she'd* been living at the time. "I cannot say," she answered with a slight harrumph.

I apologized for the interruption. Perhaps it's impolite to inquire after a yew's age.

The plants are a few years older now, still green and full as ever, with their distinctive tall and narrow shape, the branches densely packed together. A rare species and very, very old indeed.

Are you ready to track down something older still?

STORMING THE BOOKSHOP

That I for poor auld Scotland's sake
Some usefu' plan or book could make.

ROBERT BURNS

*N*ot a car has driven by since we arrived at the Urr Parish Church. Nor do we pass another vehicle as we sally forth in search of an ancient earthwork. It's called a *mote*, meaning a mound or embankment. Man-made, it features a flat-topped citadel surrounded by trenches and a broad base, perched along the Urr's west bank.

What the Mote of Urr really looks like is a dish of pudding, though the engraving in Francis Grose's *The Antiquities of Scotland* gives it the appearance of a flying saucer. Not that Grose would have known about such a thing in 1797.

Oh, the rumors that have circulated about this round mound! Some say it was an open-air courtroom for dispensing justice, others that pagans gathered here for worship and sacrifices. Still more insist a dragon encircled the mote and was slain by a knight, who covered his armor with sharp razors, then induced the dragon to swallow him. *Ugh.* The answer, according to modern archaeologists, is none of the above; instead, the mote once supported a timber tower house, dating from the twelfth century.

We turn south onto a tree-lined road with the Urr Water well in sight and search the far bank. Aye, there's the old mote, fascinating if only because of its size. It rises eighty-five feet from the base and is the most extensive site of its kind in Scotland. Especially now that it's raining again, it's difficult to get a good look at the unusual shape. I'll turn around at Netheryett, a whimsical-sounding property name that simply means lower gate.

Slowing down, we take a last gander before pressing on for Haugh of

Urr. At the crossroads again, but pointing a different direction this time, we continue on the narrow two-lane road with a forest on our left and a hedgerow on our right until we cross a burn and start to climb, taking in a fine view of the rolling farmlands.

The entrance to Spottes Hall is on our left, though the gate is closed and the house well hidden by trees. *Do the descendants of Michael Herries still live here?* I wonder. My impression is that people do far less moving around in Scotland than in America, particularly old families with old money. Considering the appealing description of this property in my guidebook—a late Georgian mansion with pavilion wings, a stable court, and a walled garden—who can blame them?

Continuing on the B794 requires a tricky dogleg across the A75, blessedly empty at this midmorning hour. Such beautiful country: hilly and winding without a straight stretch of road to be found. Not much farther and we come to the Old Bridge of Urr, nestled down a steep, curving road. According to the weathered sandstone panels featuring a lion rampant and crown, this span was built in 1580. The farm buildings clustered along the riverbanks were built two centuries later and still qualify as old. I cross the single-lane, humpback bridge just for the thrill of it, then turn around at the nearest intersection, only to drive downhill and over the stone arches again, noting properties named Mill Lade and Lea Cottage and an unusual flock of sheep: cream colored with brown spots.

BOUND FOR BENNY'S

I haven't forgotten my pledge at breakfast: to the bookshop of Benny Gillies we go. We're coming into Kirkpatrick Durham from the south on

Church Road, as pleasant an approach as any. As for the stormy weather, no use complaining; rainfall is what makes Scotland so delightfully green.

When we reach the village, a right turn onto Victoria Street takes us to Benny's wee shop. A whitewashed cottage among its gray and white neighbors, it's easily found: "Bookshop" is a sign readers and writers seldom miss. Wishing we'd brought an umbrella, we huddle in the shallow entranceway and press the bell, grateful when the royal blue door swings open seconds later.

"You made it," our genial host says, standing back to make room for us.

I rang Benny up before we left the B&B, always recommended with small, off-the-beaten-path shops. A find, isn't it? Floor to ceiling books, antiquarian maps on the walls, and a purring tabby named Masie. It's the perfect place to be on a *dreich* day like this.

"Sorry to be so wet." I fold my dripping scarf and stuff it in my jacket pocket, then shake hands with the man who's spent the last decade stocking my writing study. "Good to see you, Benny."

"And you." Sporting a neatly trimmed beard and wearing a green sweater that matches his eyes, Benny Gillies has a sharp intellect, paired with an easygoing manner and a ready smile. "Tea first, or do you want to have a look around?"

Now there's a difficult choice.

"I'll fetch a couple of mugs," he offers, sensing my dilemma. While he climbs the few stairs into his home—an adjoining two-story cottage—we catch our breath and begin perusing his wares.

Ahhh, Books

I've been in secondhand bookshops that were a jumbled mess, with stacks of books toppling along windowsills, periodicals slithering across the floor, and shelves crammed with everything from children's books to cookbooks in no certain order. That would not be Benny's shop; his bookshelves are logically organized and clearly marked. And it's all Scottish, all the time. Architecture? Right this way. Folklore? Yes, indeed. Tours and Early Travelers? Choose from Boswell, Heron, Pennant, and fifty other authors on the subject.

"Here we go." Benny returns with two steaming mugs of tea. "Milk and sugar, aye?"

I accept the offered mug and breathe in the warm scent while eying a particular volume of interest. It looks familiar. Might I already own it? With my free hand, I pull from my purse a stapled sheaf of papers listing my current Scottish titles (please don't ask how many) and squint at the small type. "Oops, I have that one." When Benny glances over my shoulder, I nod toward the shelf. "Gilhooley's *Dictionary of Edinburgh in 1752*." A reprint, of course, but still invaluable to a novelist.

While you scratch Masie the cat behind the ears, I select two dozen must-have titles from Benny's extensive collection. More than that, and my suitcase will protest. The good news? No cost for shipping if I take them with me, and when we arrive at customs in the United States, books are duty free. My husband keeps explaining the substantial difference between *free* and *duty free,* but as long as I have an armload of new old books, I'm a happy woman.

The phone rings, and Benny leaves me to my own dangerous devices in the literature section. "Lyn says hello," he calls out a minute later. His wife is off for the day, visiting their daughter near Girvan. I'm sorry Lyn's not here; not only is she an exceptional cook and a fine hostess, she also has a keen sense of adventure. Last time I visited, Benny shared photos from their trip to India, including one of Lyn riding an elephant.

You've found something to read too, I see: Ramsay's *Poems, Epistles, Fables, Satires, Elegies, and Lyrics.* Who could resist an inviting title like that?

Shopping completed and tea mugs drained, we tally up our purchases and hand over the necessary cash. I'll try not to envy your eight-pound total; as usual, my bill is significantly higher, though I consider these treasures a worthy investment.

"Where have you booked in for tonight?" Benny asks. This has nothing to do with used books; he wants to know if we've arranged our lodging.

"The Selkirk Arms in Kirkcudbright." I glance toward the window. "Since it has stopped raining, I thought we'd take the shore road by the abbey."

"Dundrennan might be muddy," he cautions, "but the light should be ideal for taking photos." He hands over my books, which fill two sacks with the PBFA logo on the side: Provincial Booksellers Fairs Association, of which Benny is a member. Naturally, the logo features a cat.

We visit a bit longer at the door, swapping family news, until his phone rings again, and we bid our genial bookseller farewell. "See you next time," I say in parting, my return certain.

A Misty Afternoon

Thick mists obscure, involv'd me round.

Robert Burns

Though a sunny day is *ferlie*—superb, or wonderful—this is the Galloway I hold close to my heart. The heavy cloud cover has lifted, a thin, wispy mist hangs in the air, and the landscape is a thousand shades of color, all of them green.

After following the A75 south to the last Castle Douglas exit, we pass Threave Gardens en route to the Kelton Parish Church. We've not far to go; there's Kirkland, a stately old stone house, on the left as we steadily climb. Our narrow, curving road guides us through a dark glade before we come to the quiet grounds of Kelton. Even on a Sabbath, it might be quiet; worshipers come here only on the third and fourth Sundays of the month.

As we step out of the car, we're greeted by the lowing of cattle from a nearby pasture. A slight breeze flutters the leaves above us; the scent is marvelous, almost sweet.

One writer called this 1805 church "a big box of harled rubble."[1] An accurate appraisal but not a sympathetic one when the simple design is so pleasing. The slender, round-arched windows speak of ecclesiastical history, and the bull's-eye windows in the gables are the perfect punctuation. Granted, the side entrance added in 1930 is awful, but if we judiciously choose our camera angles, the folks at home will see only a fine auld kirk in the most sylvan of settings.

We're not far from Rhonehouse, where the Keltonhill Fairs of long ago were held on the Tuesday nearest midsummer. What began as a horse fair—the largest in South West Scotland, drawing fairgoers from England and Ireland—became a much-anticipated event with high-spirited revelry from dawn until the gloaming. Even today, if a Scotswoman's life is crazier than usual, she'll say, "It's a Keltonhill Fair around here."

Narrow Is the Way

Good thing no one is headed to the fair down *this* wee road. As we continue toward Gelston, aware of the bushy hedgerows closing in on us, I listen for the sound of a car engine coming our direction. I never can decide which is the better method: crawl along, prepared to hit the brakes at any moment, or drive pell-mell as if I have the road to myself. I've tried both; the first is more scenic, the second adds an element of excitement.

Since I have a passenger with me, the choice is easy: sit back and drink in the scenery. Remember I told you we'd go places no motor coach would dare attempt? This is one of them.

My husband insists some Scottish roads were created by pouring asphalt on top of a hill and letting it find its own path to the bottom. Not true, though he and I did brave such a road on the Isle of Skye, leading down to the ferry at Glenelg Bay. Rather like a steep, vertical drop on a roller coaster. The kind that makes you scream even if you try not to.

Then there's the B8007 on the Ardnamurchan Peninsula, an official single-track road (which requires a one-track mind on the part of the driver). Imagine motoring in the rain at twilight with a tall stone dyke on one side, a sheer cliff overlooking a sea loch hundreds of feet below on the other, lambs wandering onto the roadway, and a car coming the other direction with no passing place in sight. Fearless driver though I may be, I was almost in tears. On the last white-knuckle stretch before reaching our B&B in Kilchoan, Bill confessed, "This is the one place that didn't fax back a confirmation…"

Our marriage survived the journey, and that memorable evening in Kilchoan was deemed the highlight of our trip, sheer relief playing a significant role.

In the Lowlands, country roads like this one serve as boundaries between farm properties, meant for moving livestock from one pasture to another or carrying oats to the miller and not at all meant for passenger cars going thirty miles per hour on a misty afternoon. That's why we're traveling at half that speed with the windows down, listening for other cars. The rain-freshened air is a bonus; so is the bleating of sheep.

We reach the crossroads at Gelston without mishap and must choose once again: a lovely woodland track along Screel Hill or a winding valley along Doach Burn on the B736? Since the B road leads directly to our next stop, we'll head northeast for a bit, then turn southeast, bound for Orchardton Tower.

FIFTEENTH ROUND

Quite as pretty as I remembered, this curvy route is squeezed between sets of hills—Torglass and Barlae, then Galgrie and Croach—before reaching the A711 and a broad, open vista with Orchardton Bay in the distance. Screel Hill on our right is towering and steep, its top devoid of trees. We can't see any water from here, but we have a sense of being nearer the shoreline. Gulls sail overhead, and the air bears a whiff of sea and salt.

Windows still rolled down, we cross the main road and press on. Despite evidence to the contrary—a bumpy road, endless farms, nothing

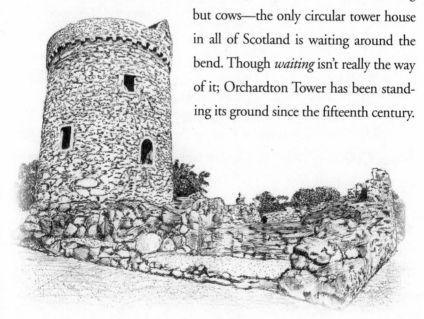

but cows—the only circular tower house in all of Scotland is waiting around the bend. Though *waiting* isn't really the way of it; Orchardton Tower has been standing its ground since the fifteenth century.

Minutes later we reach the car park, surprised to find two vehicles already there. Heavens, a traffic jam. The college-age visitors—unquestionably American—either know one another or are exceedingly outgoing. Some of them are standing in the grassy expanse beside the car park tossing a Frisbee back and forth. Others are precariously balanced on the stone walls enclosing the servants' quarters, while two more have climbed the high, round tower to the walkway and are hanging over the parapet, making me uneasy.

"Hi, Mom!" one young man calls down, grinning as he leans farther out to wave.

Taking my cue, I shout, "That's far enough, Son!" Though I'm smiling, I use my Mother-does-not-approve voice; he obediently pulls back.

In short order, the lads gather around us, curious perhaps. Or glad to hear American accents. Or missing their mums. College soccer-team members, they've landed in Scotland after their exams. "Just seeing the country," one red-headed player says with a shrug.

I eye their hired cars, knowing the minimum age requirement. "Who are the designated drivers?"

Two hands go up. "Older brothers," is the quick explanation, though they look as youthful as the rest. Since the drinking age in Scotland is eighteen, I send up a silent prayer and resist the urge to ask for their mothers' phone numbers.

Apparently they've seen enough of Orchardton Tower and start piling in their vehicles: four in one, five in another, a tight squeeze.

"Where are you headed next?" I ask, secretly hoping it's not Dundrennan; abbeys are best enjoyed in solitude.

A dark-eyed boy inclines his head toward the road. "Dumfries, if we don't get lost this time."

"Make a right onto the A711," I tell the two drivers, who nod, looking more responsible by the minute. "Follow that route all the way to the town center."

After a bit of good-natured name-calling and door slamming, the team disappears in a spray of gravel, leaving a blessed silence in their wake. I take a deep breath, then exhale, and laugh when you do the same.

Now that we have the place to ourselves—though Historic Scotland maintains this remote tower, it stands unattended—we pull out our digital cameras and start clicking away. I consider Orchardton the most photogenic castle in Galloway, especially when a slight mist settles over the scene. The setting is idyllic, nestled among fertile fields, green pastures, and softly folded hills. The castle's round shape is strikingly medieval and well preserved. Mounted inside the windows are decorative iron bars with graceful curves, framing each pastoral view.

Unlike the massive hulks of Drumcoltran and Threave, Orchardton exudes an aura of beauty, of civility. The castle wasn't simply a fortress; the Cairns family, awarded this land for helping to overthrow the Douglases, once made their home here.

And ate their meals here, you remind me, pointing to your watch.

To Auchencairn, to find a fit lunch. You'll not mind if we break bread with smugglers?

OF SMUGGLERS AND MONKS

He'll have them by fair trade,
if not, he will smuggle.

ROBERT BURNS

*T*he steep Main Street of Auchencairn lies just three miles south of Orchardton. A century ago Scottish novelist S. R. Crockett called the place a "little, bright, rose-bowered, garden-circled, seaside village."[1] All true. But it's smugglers I've tempted you with, not flowers. And lunch, posthaste.

Free traders, as smugglers of old preferred to be called, must have frequented the eighteenth-century Auchencairn Arms since it's now known as the Old Smugglers Inn. Men didn't boast about such escapades in those days; the Smuggler's Act of 1736 demanded the death penalty for anyone bearing arms against a revenue officer.

Even so, most folk in Galloway were glad to see tea, salt, candles, tobacco, claret, and other goods appear on the Solway's shores free of the steep taxes imposed by their neighbors to the south. A white sheet spread across a dark thatch roof signaled a safe landing, after which it took a small army of men and women to move the illicit cargo off the boats and across the hills and moors, dodging the excise officials. If the seamen could get past the revenue cutters by sea, the villagers reckoned they could do their part on land; to be caught was deemed the only sin in free trading. The free traders' efforts came to a profitable end miles inland—in Clachanpluck or Haugh of Urr, in Buittle or Drumcoltran.

To be honest, I don't think we'll find any smugglers here; even Old Gladys, the hostelry's resident ghost, hasn't made an appearance in some time. But if pub food will suffice, the restaurant serves until 2:00.

Inn and Out

We park in front of the two-story inn with its whitewashed exterior trimmed in reddish brown. A narrow pair of doors gives away the building's age, though the interior is freshly decorated with honey-colored wood paneling and a jazzy carpet in red, turquoise, and gold, spruced up for summer tourists who flock to the Scottish Riviera, as this stretch of coastline is locally known.

A young blonde with a ponytail swinging down her back sidles up to greet us. "Will ye be wanting food? Cook's about to clean the grill."

We glance at the menu and order on the spot—steak and kidney pie—then settle down at an empty table in the lounge bar and wonder what we're in for. "It smells delicious," I tell the waitress when she serves the deep-dish meal covered with a flaky pastry. "What's in it? I mean, besides steak and—"

"Beef kidneys, sautéed with onions, cooked in ale and meat stock." She's been asked this before. Her gaze wanders toward the door. "Will there be anything else?"

"Just a check," I tell her, which she promptly slaps on the table before tugging off her apron and heading for the kitchen.

While our pies cool, we eye the room. Two solitary patrons sit at opposite ends of the curving bar, nursing pints of lager that have long since lost their creamy heads. According to a posted notice, dinner is served on the weekends, cooked to order, and uses local produce "as far as possible." Every other Thursday night the inn offers traditional sessions with local musicians on fiddle, bodhrán, flute, and tin whistle. The memorable evening with my husband in Kilchoan included just such a session with a ragtag group featuring two accordions—three too many, Bill noted. We kept hoping they'd stop playing and have a good *argle-bargle* since their voices were more musical than their instruments.

Before long, our steak pies are enjoyed, our bottled waters emptied, and our bill paid. Some holiday meals are feasts to be remembered; others simply serve as fuel for the road, though this one was flavorful enough.

Stepping outside, we're struck with how hilly this village is and how quiet. The only sound is the lowing of cattle. Not a soul is walking up or down the two steep main streets, one of which winds upward past the lovely old parish church overlooking Auchencairn Bay.

Now that we're back on the A711 headed south, suppose I tell you an Auchencairn tale from 1695. Strange things began to occur at the Mackie farm that year. Inexplicable things. Cattle were moved; the peat stack was lit; household items went missing, then reappeared in odd places; stones were thrown at family members. Rev. Alexander Telfair and fourteen of his parishioners bore witness to the evil manifestations. When the minister tried to bless the house, clods of dirt were thrown at him by an unseen hand.

And then on May Day the attacks stopped. Though life returned to normal for the Mackies, they eventually abandoned their farmhouse, which collapsed after many years. But if you ask Auchencairn natives, they'll show you where the house once stood.

Aren't you glad I saved that chilling story until now, when the village is well behind us? And aren't you relieved that our next stop is a place where the Lord—and not the Adversary—reigns?

OLD ABBEY

Dundrennan Abbey, founded in 1142, bears little resemblance to Sweetheart Abbey. Though the monastic design follows strict Cistercian rules, the setting is markedly different, with more hills, more land, and more trees. Too, Dundrennan was made of gray stone quarried from the nearby sea cliffs instead of Sweetheart's red sandstone.

While much of Scotland feels like a sacred ruin, I think you'll find this place especially memorable.

We pass through a small wooded area, carpeted with Scottish bluebells, then find ourselves in a gentle valley, the grass around us dense and plush. If not for the stone dykes and wildflowers, I'd fear we'd driven onto a golf course by mistake.

A bridge carries us over Abbey Burn and into the diminutive village of Dundrennan, a single main street intersected by a few, short side streets. The village consists of one- and two-story cottages—no tearooms, no quaint shops, no inns. Most of the homes and a feed supply store are on the right, with only a few cottages on the left before the abbey suddenly appears. Even though I've come upon this scene many times, my eyes still water the moment I glimpse its timeless, solemn beauty.

The ruins of Dundrennan Abbey are ethereal, almost imaginary, as if the Gothic arches were hand painted on a canvas of blue green hills. The cloistered grounds are in the center of the village yet stand apart, holding the world at bay with meadows on all sides. I drive down to the gate, wishing our tires weren't so noisy on the gravel. Cistercian monks preferred secluded, untamed settings; how the twelfth-century monks and their hard-working lay brothers must have rejoiced when they first came here.

We stop in the gift shop to show our Historic Scotland passes and are surprised to discover behind the counter our modern Duncan from Sweetheart Abbey.

"Robert took ill this morning," he explains, "and since it was my day off…" He shrugs. "We help each other, ye *ken*?"

I smile at his use of the familiar Scots word. "Yes, I do know. Very thoughtful of you. And what a nice shop this is."

He shows us his wares: guides to other Historic Scotland properties, local maps, various books on Scottish history and customs, and the usual tourist trappings. Bill still wears the Dundrennan T-shirt I purchased here many springs ago.

"Been to this abbey before, have you?"

When you tell him it's your first visit, he insists on walking with us to the nave, pointing out the remains of the choir, the transepts, the presbytery, the chapter house. At Glenluce Abbey in far western Galloway, the chapter house was rebuilt in 1500, such that the walls and roof are still in place. Choral groups come from far and wide to sing in the hallowed chamber, each note suspended in the air for many seconds after it's released. I tried it myself once, singing into my little tape recorder when no one was paying attention. The effect is quite something, like singing in the world's largest shower.

With a tip of his cap, our Duncan look-alike returns to his labors, letting us explore the abbey ruins at our leisure. In the days of 35 mm film, I went through several rolls each time I walked through Dundrennan. This afternoon I pull out my digital camera, certain my Memory Stick is up to the task. We wander from arch to arch, capturing closeups of the intricate carvings and inscriptions, using the magnificent architecture to frame the gnarled trees and crumbling gravestones, the adjoining pastures and nearby hills. Even the ironwork on the gates deserves the attention of our lenses.

It'll be interesting to compare photos later; a great deal depends on lighting and angle. The stone can appear dark gray, pale gray, light brown, even golden. Bright, sunny days are my least favorite here (I realize how ridiculous that sounds), because then the grass is as green as Astroturf, the light washes out the fine details of the stone carvings, and the angle of the sun casts half the abbey in shadows.

Today is ideal, just as Benny said it would be. Enough mist lingers in the air to soften the stark, gray edges and diffuse the sounds of the modern world. Car engines aren't so loud; the dog barking in someone's garden is muted. Though the sky has lightened, it's still gray rather than a brilliant, spring blue. Dundrennan is nothing if not atmospheric; this afternoon you're seeing the abbey at her contemplative best.

NEW IN TOWN

'Twas by the banks o' bonie Dee,
Beside Kirkcudbright's towers.

ROBERT BURNS

The monks of Dundrennan would be heartbroken to learn what's happened to the land west of their beloved abbey. All along the A711, from Dundrennan to Mutehill and south to Netherlaw Point, are posted alarming signs: "Random Gun Firing!" And on the same portion of land, the O.S. map proclaims in bold red, "Danger Area," noted once in large, capital letters and ten times more in small print. No exclamation points, but we get the idea.

Here's the story: this is a firing range for the British military, where they test tanks by shooting shells into the sea. I realize they must practice *somewhere,* but did they have to choose this bucolic corner of Scotland?

Despite all those unsettling signs, it's a scenic route through the rolling countryside. Every road leading to Kirkcudbright offers a fine prospect, though this approach is my favorite. Driving down the hill toward town one May afternoon at this hour, I watched as the slanted sunlight turned the bay into a glistening, silver evening gown, pooled at Kirkcudbright's feet. Awestruck, I stopped along the shoulder of the road—not to take a photo but to catch my breath.

Now that we've reached the royal burgh, we turn left on Saint Cuthbert Street, a clue to the town's unusual name. Over time, "Kirk of Cuthbert" became one long word with a vastly different spelling and a pronunciation—"ker-COO-bree"—that stymies out-of-towners.

Kirkcudbright has a working harbor and marina right in the heart of town. Gaily colored boats bob in the water—very nautical, with all the blue, white, and red—and steady coastal breezes keep the smell of fish from permeating the air.

MacLellan's Castle is also at the center of things, as you're about to see. Oh, I love your expression! To come upon a four-story, sixteenth-century town house, complete with corbeled turrets, smack in the middle of town *is* rather remarkable, even in Scotland. I wonder if many tourists have had accidents here, slamming on their brakes when they reach Castle Street.

Kirkcudbright is definitely a walking town; we'll dispense with our car shortly. But just to get our bearings, let's drive around a bit, starting down Castle. It's not a large place—some thirty-five hundred people call it home—yet it's both an old market town and an artists' town, with granaries and creameries, art galleries and gardens. Here's the High Street, an L-shaped affair; we'll turn right for now.

On our left are a series of shops and then the Tolbooth Art Centre. Lovely old rubble building, and huge: three stories tall with a mercat cross on top of the stair. See the colorful sign for "Jo Gallant, Textile Artist"? That's our first stop in the morning.

We've turned right again, but we're still on the High Street, with its grand houses. Mostly eighteenth century, done in various pastels, roofed with dark blue slates, many with white curtains in the window. The colors remind me of Charleston, South Carolina, also an old harbor town. A "Doors of Kirkcudbright" art poster would be a natural, whether photographed or painted, since each entranceway is unique.

There's the castle again. We'll travel up Cuthbert another block, take a turn on Saint Mary, and start at the other end of the High Street, where we'll find our 1770-era hotel soon after we turn. Parking is always at a premium; let's see if we're lucky…ah!

BURNS SLEPT HERE TOO

And here's our lodging: three stories tall, painted creamy white with sage green trim and flower boxes in the windows. Very smart. The Selkirk Arms is a true hotel—Best Western, Scottish Tourist Board, Royal Automobile Club, Taste of Scotland, all that—but be not dismayed; it's still historic, friendly, and decidedly Scottish. "An old hotel abounding in antique sideboards and cupboards," declared Rev. Dick.[1]

After all, this is where Robert Burns stayed when he wrote what came to be known as "The Selkirk Grace," which ends with this couplet:

> But we hae meat and we can eat,
> And sae the Lord bethankit.

Amen to that.

The hotel entrance is around on the side, beneath the awning. When we venture through the door, luggage in hand, the young fellow at reception calls out a warm greeting (*young* being a relative term; he's probably thirty). Pressed white shirt and tie, neatly trimmed hair, and clean fingernails all make for a good impression.

"You've a reservation, aye?" His voice has that pleasant Lowland lilt, ending on the upswing. He smiles, nodding at his computer. "Indeed, here you are, Mrs. Higgs."

No one ever calls me that at home. I like the sound of it, as if I'm a stable, mature person instead of a writer.

They have sixteen bedrooms, all *en suite,* an important consideration. That means a bathroom is part of your room, and private. Otherwise your bath could be down the hall, down the stair, shared with teenagers—brother, could I tell you some stories.

As to pricing, hotels here do things differently. In the United States, you pay the same price for a hotel room whether it has one guest or two. In the United Kingdom, a single guest generally pays a premium and is given a smaller room, unless you're willing to pay even more to have what they call a "double for single occupancy"—not twice the cost, by any means, but not inexpensive. For two travelers sharing a room, the tariff quoted for double rooms is often *per person*. Once you throw in the exchange rate, a price that sounds like a bargain—"Look, only £65 for a superior double room!"—turns out to be about $240 a night. Forgive the math exercise; I just don't want you to faint when your Visa bill arrives.

And wait until we buy petrol.

"This way, if you please." Our efficient reception clerk has handed us off to a woman closer to my age, who has both bags in tow and is leading us down the hall, a room key tucked in her pocket. We're soon settled into our "superior" room—what's another fifteen pounds?—and have asked her to reserve us a table for dinner at 7:00. After our heavy lunch, seafood sounds like just the ticket. Please don't let me order dessert.

RISE AND SHINE, EVENTUALLY

No need to apologize for having a *lie-in* this morning. We've kept a good pace since we landed, and a five-hour time difference is bound to take its toll. Sir Harry Lauder, a Scottish entertainer from the last century, had it right: "Oh, it's nice to get up in the mornin' / But it's nicer to lie in bed."[2]

Besides, the shops are only now opening their doors. And isn't the weather looovely? The sun, hanging against a pale blue sky, makes an occasional appearance, then slips behind a thin layer of clouds. The temperature is ideal: we aren't missing our jackets, wishing we'd worn them, nor wearing them, wishing we hadn't.

Sidewalks are well used here. Women of various ages—dressed in skirts and jumpers, tending dogs on leashes—stand on the corners chatting away as if they had all the time in the world. We've already passed several baby *prams*, some being pushed by young mothers, others by older nannies; perhaps this is the appointed hour when infants require airing.

The sense of civility—of a daily routine, of knowing one's neighbors, of leading busy lives that still have a bit of breathing room—is appealing. But I try not to fantasize about actually *living* here. As friendly and kind as folk are, I would always be an *incomer*, a foreigner, always "the American woman." (This is not meant as criticism; if a lass from Galloway moved to Kentucky, we would welcome her with open arms. Yet her unique accent, her particular habits, her over-the-pond experiences would always mark her as "the Scottish woman.")

And so I visit Dumfries and Galloway, bask in the charming differences, leave behind as many tourist dollars as I can, and take home all the memories my heart and mind can hold. We travel not only to appreciate other places but also, when we return home, to fully appreciate our own. To see our small world through eyes opened wider by gazing up at a Scottish sky on a Thursday morning in May.

On the High Street

Reader, attend!…

Know, prudent, cautious, self-control

Is wisdom's root.

Robert Burns

You can't go wrong with a silk scarf: one size truly does fit all, scarves never go out of style, and you'd have to buy about thirty of them before your suitcase even noticed.

And that *color.* "It's a perfect match for your eyes." Jo Gallant, veteran shopkeeper and textile artist, is right: that scarf is meant to be yours.

I already have a purchase of my own, which will *not* slide into my suitcase un-noticed: a pottery bowl. You'd think I'd know better.

I once brought home a handmade wooden box from Mull that took up half my suitcase and weighed a ton. But it's a *thriftie,* you see—a money box—and so it has sentimental value, as any reader who wanted to see fictional Lachlan McBride get his comeuppance will understand. Another time I hauled home a footman made of…I don't know…some heavy metal. Tin-plated iron, Bill says. It took up *more* than half my suitcase, and I had some explaining to do at customs. What was it, exactly? And did it qualify as an antiquity?

According to the saleswoman at the Edinburgh antique shop, a gentleman of the late eighteenth century would prop his feet on this by the fire, or the lady of the house might use it to keep her teakettle warm. An antique, yes, but not an antiquity. Since I don't start fires in my writing study, all my footman does is hold the wooden box.

"Enjoy the fine weather," Jo trills as we leave her colorful abode.

And we do enjoy the weather for about thirty seconds until we walk into the next shop, a custom jeweler whose intricate work we quickly realize we cannot possibly afford. After looking about, not wanting to offend, we hasten back to the sidewalk and cross the street, as if we'd stumbled through his door by mistake.

Not far around the bend is a sizable shop with "Osborne Antiques" beside the door. Perfect. We can browse all we like and buy nothing, without offending someone's artistry. Or fall in love with a seven-foot grandfather clock, as I did while shopping near Melrose Abbey in the Scottish Border country. I ran my fingers along the wooden case, pictured it in my writing study, and tried to figure the exchange rate in my head, before reason prevailed. I stepped back, knowing I had absolutely no way of getting such a thing home without breaking the clock or breaking the bank.

I fear I will not show that kind of restraint here at Osborne's. They have antique linens; I have a friend who adores linens. Good news: they take up almost no room, and because they're secondhand items, they're also duty free. As far as U.S. Customs is concerned, I have yet to spend a dime. Well, except for the earrings from Abbey Cottage. And the pottery bowl.

"Thank you for your custom, mem." The gentleman waiting on us looks older than anything in the shop. His back is bent like a willow rocker, and the glasses sliding down his nose resemble Ben Franklin's, the thin wires barely circling around his large ears. He has all his teeth, though, and an endearing smile. "Will there be anything else?"

I stay my hand from clasping the sterling-silver letter opener fetchingly displayed on a red velvet cloth. Alas, I do *not* need a letter opener for e-mail. And so, with a heavy sigh, I leave with naught but my friend's linens. And the pottery bowl.

FOR ART'S SAKE!

A gallery should keep us out of trouble. Either the artwork is not for sale, or it's so expensive that only well-to-do English tourists can afford it.

Kirkcudbright became home to a colony of artists from Glasgow in the waning years of the nineteenth century. The softness of the light drew them, some said. The rugged Galloway scenery, the fishing boats in the harbor, the myriad colors of the houses—everything an artist could desire is here. Once a few came, more joined them; hence the designation as an artists' town. The Harbour Cottage Gallery at the end of the High Street has the added bonus of being on the waterfront. Their hours are a bit *wonky*, though; I think if we walk quickly, we'll just make it.

Moments later, breathless but ahead of the 12:30 closing time, we dart through the brightest of blue doors into an airy space filled with contemporary paintings and crafts created by local artists. It's a fine exhibit, though I confess my taste runs more to the old masters.

After a brief visit we're politely eased out the door into the afternoon sunlight. If I knew how to hold a paintbrush, I would set up an easel right here along the banks of the River Dee and paint Greyfriars Scottish Episcopal Church—built one century at a time, it seems, beginning with the fifteenth. Made of gray stone rubble, the steep-roofed sanctuary is a pleasing jumble of angles and finials and Gothic, stained-glass windows. Overlooking the harbor, the church is surrounded by beautiful old shade trees. Near the front door rests a striking red bench. Surely an artist must have placed it there.

Across the street is the castle of the day. MacLellan's has nothing in common with Threave except the word *castle*. The latter is a fortress, built to intimidate the neighbors; the former is a town house, meant to impress them. After the Reformation, local landowner Sir Thomas MacLellan of Bombie acquired the property and began his ambitious building project. Tradition has it the upper rooms were never finished, the family fortune was soon squandered, and MacLellan's Castle was abandoned by the early 1700s.

Here's what's left: a graceful ruin, ready to be explored by yet another pair of tourists. We stroll around to the ticket shop on the far corner of the property, our walk brightened by a border of pink and white tulips. Behind the counter stands a thirtysomething woman with big, brown cow eyes and the long lashes to go with them.

When we pull out our Historic Scotland passes and a dog-eared guidebook I brought from home, she blinks at us. "Welcome back, eh?"

MacLellan's is an easy castle to explore. No hiking or boating is required; we simply enter through the keystone archway. Looking around the ground-floor kitchen, I listen for the faint echo of banging pots or shouting cooks and instead hear hollow voices from the laird's *lug,* a not-so-secret hiding place where Sir Thomas could eavesdrop on his guests through a small spy hole in the back of the great hall's fireplace.

A couple emerges from the shadowy chamber, each bearing a toddler. Twins, I'd say. With their curly black hair, the lads are the image of their father. Pulling one child closer, the mother says in a stage whisper, "I didn't hear anything through the lug, Tommy. Did you?"

Her son nods and points at us, then sticks his finger in his mouth to be safe.

We all chuckle, then she asks, "On holiday, are you?"

Sunshine pours through the square window grates as we engage in small talk while the toddlers wiggle and squirm. "We're from Carlisle," the young man offers. "I work with computers. Nancy here is a homemaker, and a good one. Got her hands full, she does."

His praise sounds sincere; all three women smile at him warmly.

They've come to Kirkcudbright for a short break, and so we leave them with a recommendation: "If you've not been to Orchardton Tower, the children would love that one. It's round and has lots of grass for running about."

"You'd fancy that part, wouldn't you, Danny?" Nancy reaches over to tickle Tommy's brother, provoking a giggle.

The family wanders out the door as we finish our self-guided tour. Because these old castles are roofless and therefore devoid of furnishings, such explorations do not take long. MacLellan's Castle is best viewed from across the street, where the photo ops are numerous. Unlike flat-sided Threave, this building is an L-plan gone wild, with additional projecting towers in two places and several tall chimneys. Leafy branches from nearby trees, some of them flowering, add a touch of color to the scene. For dreamy photos that look like postcards, MacLellan's in May is romantic Scotland at its best.

HOME AND GARDEN

Now that it's past 1:00, Broughton House will be open. Suppose we swing by the car and deposit our packages to spare my dropping the pottery bowl. Or wearing it on my head. (The urge to turn every concave object into a hat is a lifelong obsession. In several bridal-shower photos, I'm wearing colanders, Dutch ovens, mesh baskets, Tupperware. Some things aren't worth trying to figure out.)

You'll recall we drove up Castle Street yesterday; now we'll get a better look. Though the High Street gets all the attention, Castle boasts some colorful houses too. Light blues and pale yellows predominate, with an occasional pastel pink, or whitewashed stone with neutral trim and a bright door. Compact cars face either direction along the curb—a standard practice in Europe, where any parking space is a good space.

After we pause so I can tuck my pottery bowl into the boot of our car, we head back toward the harbor, passing one inviting close after another: Cannon's Close, MacLellan's Close, Town Walls Close. These enclosed stone passageways shoot off at right angles, leading to gardens and courtyards that look most intriguing. The narrow side streets of Kirkcudbright have interesting names too: Tarpits Lane, Pipers Court, Corby Slap.

And here's Broughton House, a first-class museum where my National Trust for Scotland card will come in handy. A noble property, isn't it? Salmon-colored stone trimmed in gray with a white fanlight over the door. E. A. Hornel, a painter of some renown, lived here in the early twentieth century. His library is worth a good look, lined as it is with bookcases containing many antiquarian gems. But Hornel's garden is what makes this place worth the price of admission.

The first thing we notice when we step outside is the birdsong, high and melodious. Flat, irregularly shaped stones create paths through the walled garden, which overlooks the River Dee. You can hear the flow of the water, low and soothing. A profusely blooming lilac, warmed by the midday sun, fills the air with its gentle fragrance.

At our feet, low, boxy hedges—mere inches high—border the walks. Beyond them the gardens are densely planted and richly green. Color is used judiciously, as we might expect in a garden designed by a painter.

One corner is filled with myriad ferns and a single Japanese maple, a splash of dark red in a sea of bright green.

We happily claim an empty bench, sitting down to admire the flowers. Come Saturday afternoon, this place will be overflowing with visitors. Thank goodness we're here on a Thursday and can sit in silence. And listen. And think. We're not entirely alone; bees are everywhere, buzzing about—but they're here for the flowers, not us.

Once we resume our stroll, we discover a Japanese section, with flowing water, a vernacular bridge, and beautifully arched trees with bright yellow blooms dripping from their slender branches. And here's a collection of pink flowers; how I wish I knew the species to tell you. Bright magenta petals on tall, bare stems. Pale lavender clusters with slender leaves. Tiny pink flowerets exploding in a bushy array. Planted among them a touch of white, a sprinkle of yellow.

My mother would love it here. Indeed, she *is* here, walking these paths with me, if only in my heart. We circle the garden a second time, wanting to see it all again, filling up our memory banks as well as our cameras.

And here's the door back into the house. Tell me, are you feeling *peckish* yet? I know a place not far along Saint Cuthbert Street that serves Cream o' Galloway ice cream. And did I mention it's right next to a bookshop?

MAKING HISTORY

Here History paints with elegance and force
The tide of Empire's fluctuating course.

ROBERT BURNS

*Y*ou knew we'd visit the bookshop first. Maybe if I hadn't glanced in the window…

Never mind. After so many days together, you are fully aware of my weaknesses.

Solway Books carries both new titles and secondhand books. Nice and bright, the shop is bigger than it appears from the outside, with a generous display of regional titles near the register. And will you look at this! Clothbound reprints of Rev. Dick's *Highways and Byways in Galloway and Carrick*. A bargain at fifteen pounds—

Did you just snatch that out of my hands? Humph. If you won't let me buy that book for you, I have another title in mind. Amuse yourself while I inspect the fiction shelves. Feel free to pet their friendly orange feline, if you can find him.

When I pay for my purchase, I learn the sorry news.

"That cat died, I'm afraid," the salesclerk tells us. "A ginger tom. We called him the Town Cat. Traveled in and out of all the shops along the street, he did. There's a memorial statue next to the Tourist Information Centre."

A statue…to a *cat*? Our next stop, then. Right after lunch.

Minutes later we're back on Saint Cuthbert, walking all of twenty steps to the threshold of Solway Tide, a tearoom dressed in bright Mediterranean hues of green and orange. Two large windows and the wide-open glass door let us enjoy the pedestrian parade, while contemporary jazz music tickles our ears.

ORANGE YOU HUNGRY?

"We've two soups today," our petite waitress informs us, putting menus in our hands. "Carrot and carrot." She grins, and no wonder. Her *hair* is the color of carrots. That is to say, really and truly orange, and not from a bottle. It's dazzling.

I can't resist teasing her. "Didn't you say there were two soups?"

"Aye." The grin widens. "Carrot and coriander. Or carrot and orange."

The second one sounds more like dessert, which prompts me to ask, "But do you have carrot *cake*?"

The Solway Tide does not. But they do have banoffee pie, a British bananas-and-toffee treat, which I order at once, and something called lemon lush pie, which you pounce upon like a rabbit offered…well, a carrot.

We both try the coriander soup, aromatic and creamy, served with a homemade roll and the usual slab of Galloway butter. Our pies taste as good as advertised, and we are soon sipping the last of our tea and sighing with contentment.

"A present for you." I hand over a Dorothy L. Sayers detective novel set in the town in which we're lodging. "The opening line is a peach: 'If one lives in Galloway, one either fishes or paints.'"[1]

"*Five Red Herrings,* is it?" Our waitress angles her head to study the cover, hands on her hips. "I keep meaning to read that."

"Very entertaining," I encourage her, resisting the temptation to say, "You *live* here, and you haven't read *Five Red Herrings*?" After all, how many good novels have been set in the Bluegrass State that I've never purchased, let alone read? I nod toward the sign at the counter. "What's the story with Cream o' Galloway ice cream?"

"It's organic," she explains. "And it's fresh. The dairy farm is over in Gatehouse of Fleet."

That much I know. One warm September afternoon, sailing along the A75, I saw a sign for Cream o' Galloway and thought, *Sure, I could go for a dip of ice cream.* The farm itself is not on the main route but well signposted: follow this country road for a wee while, then turn left down this other road for another half mile. Which I did—or tried to—until I hit a line of traffic that suggested free diamonds were being handed out at the top of the hill.

Vehicles were abandoned willy-nilly along the steep farm road. Dogs on leashes were barking out their favorite flavors. (At least that's what it sounded like to me.) Families with big smiles were coming down the hill licking ice cream cones; others were just coming down the hill, not at all happy. I lowered my window, hoping for information.

"The queue wraps clear round the building," one stout fellow grumbled. The children behind him had very sad faces.

Mine was sad too. No Cream o' Galloway that day.

Our carrot-haired waitress must have noticed the wistful look in my eyes. "Have ye never tasted it?" In hospitable Scots fashion, she brings us each a cool spoonful of Luxury Vanilla.

Mmm. Now I understand why the road to Rainton Farm was lined with cars. "Do they have other flavors?"

Do they! Caramel Shortbread. Sticky Toffee. Whisky, Honey, and Oatmeal. Heather Cream. And another Scottish flavor you'll need to try before we fly, based on a farmhouse favorite called *cranachan*.

We quickly stand and gather our things, lest she make us a flavorful offer we can't resist, and bolt out the door, calling out our thanks.

AULD FASHIONED

The air is milder, and the harbor does smell like fish after all, though not unpleasantly so. We make a beeline for the Tourist Centre in search of a cat statue and find it easily enough: an oval stone plaque stating the particulars—Ceasar "The Town Cat," 1990–2004—including a Web site with the amusing name of www.ceasarspalace.co.uk. In front of it stands a white statue of Ceasar perched on a black marble and red sandstone pedestal. The cat's meow, don't you think?

After duly paying our respects, we continue along Saint Cuthbert

Street, crowded with practical shops not meant for gadabout tourists: an *ironmonger's,* a launderette, a paint store. Once we turn onto Saint Mary—also the A711, hence broader and busier than the other streets in town—our attention is drawn to a sporting event in progress. The members of the Kirkcudbright Bowling Club are rolling on the green.

We scurry across the street, then do our best to appear nonchalant as we inch along the sidewalk, watching a group of retirement-age gentlemen compete in their sport of choice. Before visiting Scotland, I thought "Bowling Green" was a city in Kentucky or a Top 40 hit by the Everly Brothers (1967, if you were wondering). Now I know lawn bowling is a sport loved all over the world and dominated by Scots.

For these traditionalists, cardigan sweaters and loose-fitting pants are de rigueur. The playing surface is a perfectly flat, perfectly green rectangle of grass, mowed with such precision we can see the diagonal pattern. (I have a friend who vacuums her plush carpet that way. Says she likes the symmetry of it.)

In lawn bowling, the grass may be symmetrical, but the balls—called bowls—are not. Instead they are slightly flattened on one side to skew the balance, preventing them from rolling in a predictably straight line. The goal is to roll them as close as possible to a smaller white ball—ideally, closer than one's opponent. How serious are British lawn bowlers? Sir Francis Drake insisted on finishing his game of bowls before setting sail to confront the Spanish Armada. Serious, then.

We stand and watch a bit longer, having given up on the nonchalant approach, until I check my watch and realize the Stewartry Museum closes in less than an hour. Back across Saint Mary Street we go, headed for a unique spot, purpose-built more than a century ago.

The British term *chockablock* must have been coined when a visitor stepped into the Stewartry Museum; back home we'd say the place is flat full. And why not when you have such a great collection? Stuffed birds, bagpipes, tricornered hats, a nineteenth-century witness box, a hunk of stone bearing a prehistoric cup and ring carving, and eighteenth-century communion tokens from all the surrounding parishes. This is a real museum, like a highly organized attic crammed with fascinating memorabilia. I feel like an explorer, as if discoveries are still being made in this museum. As if at any given moment a visitor might exclaim, "So *that's* where it went!" or "Has anyone seen *this* before?"

The wooden cases, many with wavy glass from an earlier era, lend a traditional, late-Victorian sensibility: formal, yet warm, not antiseptic. Inside each glass-topped case is information not easily found in libraries. For example, I own an excellent book on Scottish wildflowers, which divides them by topography, such as roadsides and hedgerows or grasslands and meadows. But here I can find out what I really need to know: which flowers bloom when in Kirkcudbrightshire? The list inside this glass case provides my answer. Interesting how well the flower names suit their given months: snowdrops in chilly January; narcissus in lovesick February; in March, slender speedwell of the genus *Veronica*, the woman who, according to legend, wiped the face of Christ as he walked to Calvary; in fresh-start April, primrose, or "first rose"; wild hyacinth for the free-spirited month of May; and round, yellow globeflowers for sunny June.

I've learned more about Galloway in this museum than in dozens of books, simply because I can study things in person. Take notes. Draw sketches. Ask questions of the curator. Where else can you see the earliest surviving sports trophy in Britain, the long, slender *Siller* (that's silver)

Gun presented by King James VI after a shooting competition? Or a great wheel for spinning wool, the sort used by Miss Sarah Wilson of Carsphairn, the last spinner in the Glenkens? Or the pulpit canopy, beneath which Rev. Dr. Thomas Blacklock—a blind minister, poet, and friend of Robert Burns—once preached?

Dear me, your eyes are glazed over. Too much history? Fair enough. We can poke around here until they close the doors, then stroll through town and tarry at all the garden gates. Later, when the birds begin their evening song, we'll buy a takeaway cup of Cream o' Galloway, find an open bench on the harbor, and wait for the gloaming.

OVER THE HILL

She thro' the whins, an' by the cairn,
An' owre the hill gaed scrievin.

ROBERT BURNS

Despite how the above verse sounds, we aren't leaving town screaming. *Scrievin* means we're gliding along easily, an ideal description of our Friday morning exit, passing the remnants of the *meikle yett,* or great gate, which once guarded the entrance to old Kirkcudbright.

Come to think of it, there *was* some muffled screaming when we stopped for petrol. First when we saw the sign "No Naked Lights." (The teenager at the pump explained that meant no open flames, like from a lighter. Oh.) And another wee scream slipped out when we paid for our fuel: forty pounds, or about seventy-five dollars, to fill a car with a smallish tank.

Alas, this isn't a recent development; our British friends have been paying higher fuel prices for ages. Now you see why we've yet to pass an SUV on the road. And why in the U.K. one hundred miles is a long distance.

A sharp left on Bridge Street carries us over the River Dee on a structure with "no pretension to prettiness"[1] yet with enough concrete to get us where we're going. Up we climb, traveling through some rugged farmland. Not rocks and boulders, just lumpy, uneven ground, as if this were the site of a fierce battle and the defeated English soldiers were left where they fell, ignobly covered with dirt. (I write fiction, remember; *Scottish* fiction.)

Overhead, we've an interesting sky this morning: brooding clouds, thick but not dark. Perhaps the sort of day that inspired the phrase "Grey Galloway." The temperature is cooler than yesterday by a few degrees. We may see a sprinkle of rain later, but we always have our scarves. And a bowl.

All at once sunlight breaks through the cloud cover, creating a bold, silvery shaft, as if Excalibur has been pulled from Loch Arthur's depths. I slow the car but don't bother to reach for my camera; phenomena like these disappear in an instant. We enjoy every second of it until the clouds shift and the shaft of light disappears.

Before driving on, I check my watch. Is it only 10:20? I never have a proper sense of time here. Either because the sun is hidden or because it travels in a lower arc, my internal light meter is useless. Nine in the morning feels like noon feels like teatime. Perhaps that's why the days seem delightfully longer. And why I seldom remember to eat lunch until 2:00, though it could be the Full Scottish Breakfasts. Aye, it definitely could be that.

We've changed maps; Landranger 84 has been filed away, and 83 is in hand. Heading north, following an unnamed yellow squiggle on the map, I brake again for another truly astonishing sight: an entire field of bunnies, their tiny brown ears and cotton white tails flicking through the grass. Look at them all! Do you suppose they plant them here, like oats?

I do believe that's the finest wildlife exhibit we've seen since we landed. Most creatures here are nocturnal, like hedgehogs, or they hide among the trees, like roe deer. Red squirrels are more common, especially in coniferous forests, while gray squirrels didn't find their way to Galloway until the nineteenth century. (Oh, the things I learned at the Stewartry Museum.)

You've been hoping to see Scottish heather—other than the packaged kind in gift shops, that is. And you *have* seen it, all over the hills, without knowing it. In late spring it's green, a low, bushy shrub covering the ground in large patches. Come July, in the drier moorlands bell heather starts to bloom. On the hills, *ling* casts a reddish purple blush across the mountains through August and September. As autumn unfolds, it fades to a darker, duskier purple and then to brown. What surprised me when I first touched heather was how soft it feels, like feathers. And heather shows up in everything, from soap to honey to ale to ice cream. So far, I can vouch for the first two.

Approaching a crossroads, we're given a choice: Tongland to the right, Twynholm to the left, the better choice as we head west toward Gatehouse of Fleet, where we'll spend the night.

FROM HERE TO THERE

What a change from flat riverbed farmland! Mature, deciduous trees crowd the curving road as we climb toward Twynholm. I've found as many explanations for the unusual name as I have different spellings. If you simply ask for "TWY-num," folk will point the way.

More old trees line the right side of the road, and then we have a clear view of the Twynholm Parish Church, sitting high above the village on a triangle of land. Built of rubble in 1818, this bonny house of worship is younger than some we've seen, older than most. Gravestones, as usual, surround the church, and a broad drive leads to the green front door, though an iron gate keeps us from turning in.

Another hill rises on the other side of Twynholm, well within view. The main road goes straight down from the church, crosses a burn, and then swings up the other side. A hundred winters ago, before automobiles got in the way, I imagine the wee lads and lassies of Twynholm had fun sledding on this stretch—or *sledging,* as it's called here.

The street has two names: Kirk Brae takes us downhill from the kirk, and Burn Brae takes us uphill from the stream. Ingenious in a two-hilled town where saying something was simply "on the brae" wouldn't help much. Small, stone cottages, most of them built in the nineteenth century, nestle close to one another. No pastel exteriors, no endless flower boxes, no putting on airs. After parking our car, down we go on foot toward the bridge at the bottom, noticing how quiet the village is. Not even the

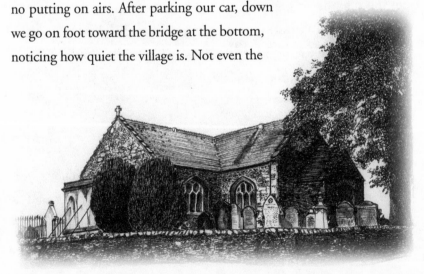

sound of a late-morning chat show on the *telly* floats through an open
window.

Captains Brae angles off to the left, taking my imagination with it.
What is it about narrow lanes disappearing around corners or over hills or
into woods that makes me want to follow them, seeing where they might
lead? Oh, the places I've ended up! I keep buying smaller and smaller cars,
not only for fuel efficiency, but also because they're easier to turn around
when I end up pulling into someone's driveway or gazing over a steep
embankment.

A few Twynholm residents have sheep or chickens in their gardens;
we can't see them yet, but we hear them. Interesting that a village with a
population of less than six hundred has not one but two public houses—
the Burnbank and the Star. We've reached the top of Burn Brae; my old-
lady knees are telling me so. (I am not old, of course, but these knees are
ancient.)

If we keep walking, we could reach Gatehouse in six miles…

Okay, we'll just start back down the hill.

FROM THERE TO HERE

I like facing this direction better, if only because we can admire the church.
The bell tower is especially nice, though it's only been here for a century.

I once attended a worship service in Twynholm. The interior is lovely:
stained-glass windows; honey-colored wooden pews in rows, with a little
shelf projecting from the back of each so you can rest your open hymnary
in front of you; one dignified box pew with velvet-lined seats and a large
square table in the center.

When I was told the pew belonged to "the woman at the big house," I smiled and bit my tongue. In the States, "the big house" is the last place you'd want to end up: a penitentiary! But here in Britain, the big house is just that: the largest estate in the parish, owned by the family who owns the parish or at least exerts considerable sway. The heritors, as they were once known.

The box pew remained empty, but forty other parishioners were on hand—all gracious, all curious. At the end of the service that day, a friendly woman came up and extended her hand. "Are you the American writer staying in Kirkcudbright?" When my mouth fell open, she hurried to add, "I'm friends with Jackie at the B&B."

News travels quickly in Galloway.

Now then, suppose we take the Old Military Road west to Gatehouse. Not as speedy as the A75 but more interesting. We'll start out on this narrow road with the hedgerow on one side and sheep on the other and a pretty burn running alongside. Up and down, up and down, but mostly up. Before long, we cross the main road and start climbing in earnest. A farm named Auchengassel is off to the right. If you're wondering, as I did, about all the names that begin with *auchen,* it simply means "field," from the Gaelic *achadh.* At least that's what Sir Herbert Maxwell wrote,[2] and who am I to argue with a baronet?

FAIR ANWOTH

Ye holy walls, that, still sublime,
Resist the crumbling touch of time.

ROBERT BURNS

We're in farm country now. Even with the windows up, the
smell is pungent. Signs at the ends of farm roads help us follow along on the map: Muiryard, Greenslack, Littleton. Very exposed
country up here, but aren't the mountains ahead glorious? At Townhead
we descend to cross a small bridge, then climb again until we reach a T in
the road, and a ferlie green T it is.

A massive stretch of woodlands, still dressed in the
many greens of summer, forced the road to veer north.
It could only be Cally Park, a thousand acres of gardens

and orchards surrounding Cally House, home to the
man who owned Girthon Parish and all it contained.

Whence Came a Prince

The man who once owned Girthon Parish was James Murray of
Broughton, a member of Parliament and a gentleman of both means and
taste. His estate house, Cally Palace—now an upmarket hotel—was
"among the largest, and most princely, in the south of Scotland"[1] when it
was built in the eighteenth century. The Murrays filled their home with
expensive furnishings, fine art, and a French chef.

We turn north, skirting the park. The tall stone wall on our left
encloses the estate, making it difficult to catch a glimpse of Cally Palace,
though the entrance gate alone is imposing. Unfortunately, most of the
thousand-acre parkland has been swallowed up by the Forestry Commission for commercial use, though the remaining acres, including a golf
course, are still lovely.

Down we go, curving toward the Water of Fleet and the burgh named
for it, Gatehouse of Fleet. Most of the time we'll hear it called simply
Gatehouse, one of the two burghs we'll visit included in *The Most Beautiful Villages of Scotland*.[2] The other we'll save for our Sunday drive in the
country.

A few teasing glimpses through the trees, then at last we're in the town
proper, greeted by a sizable clock tower, built in 1871 and deemed "predictably wild" by one writer.[3] Honestly, it seems fairly tame to me, though
architecturally speaking, the belfry does have a rather over-the-top, post-
medieval look to it, with a parapet, of all things—no doubt to protect
mice from tumbling to their deaths.

The gray Victorian clock tower sits amid the much older posting stables on our right and the two-story Murray Arms Hotel on our left. Attractive, isn't it, with its freshly whitewashed stone and that elaborate blue and red crest over the side door? As old as Cally itself—having once served as the gatehouse for the estate—the Murray Arms has grown into a twelve-room hotel, full of nooks and crannies and alcoves and half stairs and long windows and high ceilings and a public room where Robert Burns wrote "Scots, Wha Hae," the unofficial national anthem of Scotland.

In other words, the Murray Arms is wonderful.

We'll return here for the night after we see more of Gatehouse, one of my favorite spots in Galloway. But then you've heard *that* before.

Vacant storefronts on the High Street are disheartening, yet we note plenty of going concerns too: Stark Chemist, Fergusson Drapers and Outfitters, the Bank of Fleet Hotel, Galloway Lodge Preserves, and in an old church the Franca Bruno Company—two rooms of designer jewelry, Celtic goods, and collectibles from far-flung places. Franca, as exotic looking as her name, is a bright light in Gatehouse, having served as the burgh's provost. I met her years ago at a craft fair and own more of her wonderful earrings than I can count.

The Anwoth Hotel, where Dorothy Sayers took up lodging while doing research for *Five Red Herrings*—set in Gatehouse as well as Kirkcudbright—has reverted to its original name, the Ship Inn. In the foreword of her novel Sayers wrote, "We shall come back next summer to eat some more potato-scones at the Anwoth."[4] Must have been tastier than the ones you and I have eaten to date: triangular and flat, lukewarm, almost lost beneath the sautéed mushrooms. The old cottage recipes call for the scones to be slathered with butter, rolled up, and served piping hot…

Uh-oh. The wistful expression on your face tells me it's nearing noon. I know just the place we can eat *and* shop. In fact, we'll park there now, at Galloway Country Style, and explore the town on foot before we see about lunch, starting with this fine old bridge a few steps west of the car park.

A Floral Surprise

Trees and tall shrubs arch over the smooth, glassy surface of the Water of Fleet. Farther down, the water begins to ripple and swirl as the Fleet turns south, headed for Fleet Bay and the Solway beyond it.

Once you've had a good look, we'll start uphill, because I have a treat for you. Not a shop, not a museum, and not lunch, though I haven't forgotten. See the Victorian arch in red sandstone a little farther up the High Street? The one that reads "Town Hall"?

My, my, where *did* that building go? To the rubble pile, I imagine, leaving only this graceful remnant to mark the entrance into Garries Park. I first discovered this garden paradise in late September. Red, pink, and white roses were blooming like mad. Even outdoors, the heady fragrance was almost overwhelming.

Stunning, isn't it? The graceful statue of the lass with the water jars in the elevated garden adds the perfect human touch. True, she *is* made of stone, but her stance is quite natural. Smaller flower beds, enclosed by miniature hedgerows like the ones at Broughton House, surround the statue, while the four stone boundary walls frame beds full of roses and annuals and roses and perennials and roses.

Even now, before the roses begin blooming, this place is a sight to behold.

Not many benches, though. I wonder if people sit on the low brick ledge that surrounds the center. If so, I'd bring a sack lunch here every day. The broad, open gates at the far end lead to Cally Park. Tempting, although a small sign cautions about wet ground and proper footwear. I keep meaning to buy a pair of Wellies while I'm here. If I can tote home a thrifite and footman, surely I can find room for large rubber boots.

Oh, dear. Your stomach growled, didn't it?

Forgive me for making you wait. Back downhill we go to Galloway Country Style. Rather touristy, but they have a great selection of salads and sandwiches and desserts, including the carrot cake we hoped for yesterday. You'll find the shop in the back has an interesting mix of clothing and collectibles, not at all the typical fare.

Was that a second growl? We'll hurry.

KILTS TO GO

Feeling better now that you've had a bite of lunch? I knew you'd find J$_2$O tasty. Those slender bottles of orange juice and passion fruit are so refreshing. When my son visited Scotland with me, he couldn't get enough of a

Glasgow-bottled soda called IRN-BRU—pronounced "iron brew"—which he describes as Orange Crush meets Big Red cream soda.

Galloway Country Style has an interesting layout: one very large room with a casual cafeteria-style restaurant, another section with quality clothing and gifts, and a kilt shop. Want to peek at the clan tartans?

We eye the fabric samples in a book from one of Scotland's many weavers and are struck by the dizzying array of colors. Admittedly, some of the patterns are pure fabrication (pun intended), created with care but *created* nonetheless, not based on historical evidence. From the sixteenth through the eighteenth centuries, Highlanders kilted themselves in lengths of woven plaid, which served as clothing by day and bedding by night. In the nineteenth century Sir Walter Scott, among others, promoted the wearing of tartan to boost national pride, and an entire industry was born.

This shop stitches up made-to-measure Highland dress, including trousers—or *trews*—waistcoats, and short or long skirts for women. Scotsmen rent kilts like American men rent tuxedos, hence the sign posted by the register: "Don't Hire, Aim Higher."

The woman behind the counter—*Kate,* her nametag says—adjusts her glasses to get a better look at us. Her brown hair is pulled back in a smooth knot, and she is nattily attired in a white blouse and kilted skirt. "Are you interested in a particular tartan?"

Good question. If you're not Scottish and don't have a clan name, can you properly wear a tartan? I hold up a swatch of wool in maroon red, forest green, and white. "My grandmother was a Crawford, but I'm not sure it's *this* Crawford."

"Was she a descendant of Sir Reginald de Crawford of Ayrshire?" she

asks brightly, reaching for an order pad. "Late thirteenth century?"

I long to answer with an emphatic yes, knowing that Margaret Crawford of that lineage married Malcolm Wallace and birthed a national hero—aye, *Braveheart* himself, Sir William Wallace. Unfortunately, our family tree has only been uprooted to the early seventeenth century. "I can't say. Not absolutely."

Kate is crestfallen. "I see."

"But am I permitted to *wear* a kilted skirt in the Crawford tartan? You know, just in case I *am* related to Sir Reginald?"

"Ehhhmmm." This is a particularly Scottish sound she is making. Much more intelligent sounding than "Uhhhh," though it serves the same purpose. "The truth is…" Whatever she is about to say, it must be bad news; she has put aside her order pad. "In Scotland, a clan tartan should only be worn by those entitled to do so. Have you perhaps taken the Crawford name?" When I shake my head, a look of resignation settles over her. "'Twould be best if you wore the Royal Stewart." A common, bright red pattern, the sort used for blankets and paper plates. "Or you might care to look at one of the modern tartans…"

"Another time," I say, stepping back. What I should have said was "Ehhhmmm," but that as well is best done by a native Scot.

We drift over to the gift shop, followed by another kilted clerk.

"Dinna mind Kate," she says in a low voice, glancing over her shoulder. "Times have changed. Anyone is welcome to wear tartan now." With a wink, she adds, "If ye've Crawfords in yer family, ye should wear yer pattern with pride."

How good to know I can don the colors of my adopted homeland without fear of folk getting their *sporrans* in a knot.

At the moment our attire is well suited for a walk in the woods. Two miles west of here are the crumbling remains of a place so far off the beaten path, few tourists bother to find it. We'll not be counted among them.

PERMANENT RENOWN

Odd how very straight this road looked on the map. Not that I'm complaining. A meandering route is far more enjoyable, especially one that climbs through a dense and deciduous wood like Killiegowan. Think what this drive must be like in autumn, when the leaves explode with color. Even now, the uncultivated grandeur of the place takes my breath away.

With all the hills and bends, it's hard to tell if another car might be coming our direction. Better roll down our windows. Ooh, chilly. And no wonder, shady as it is. The air grows lighter as we ease downhill toward our destination and leave our dark, cool woods behind.

Finding a parking place is not difficult in this secluded clearing surrounded by meadows and woods and birds and sky and little else. A charming cottage sits across the way: the former Anwoth schoolhouse, built in the early nineteenth century (making it practically new).

Across the road, nestled in a curve, is the old Anwoth Kirk, erected in 1627.

Enclosed by a dry stane dyke and surrounded by trees,
the preaching house was a simple rectangle of gray
stone with a belfry high above the door and a steeply
pitched roof.

Whence Came a Prince

The ruins of Anwoth Kirk look like many others scattered across Galloway. Buittle, Kelton, Rerrick, Tongland, Girthon, Kirkmabreck, Monigaff—I've made pilgrimages to each, and to be honest, if I tossed the photos in a heap, I might have a hard time telling them apart were it not for their unique settings. Each one is a rubble rectangle, like this one. Roofless but unashamed. Open to the heavens. Exposed to the elements yet still standing.

What sets Anwoth apart is this engraved panel over the door, extolling the virtues of Samuel Rutherford, minister to his "Fair Anwoth by the Solway" from 1627 to 1638. Can you read the small print? "Preacher of Permanent Renown: Reformer and Defender of the Faith."

His tireless labor in this parish was legendary, drawing the unwelcome attention of King Charles. Rutherford was banned from his pulpit for his nonconformist views regarding the separation of church and state, then banished to Aberdeen, where he was not permitted to preach. Instead he wrote hundreds of letters, which traveled throughout Scotland, encouraging his brethren. They were collected and published shortly after his death, without an editor or publisher named on the title page, so great was the risk in those unsettled times. His famous letters are still in print, still uplifting the faithful.

Four centuries is a fine start on permanent renown.

CASTLE AND CAIRN

Sae in the tower o' Cardoness
A howlet sits at noon.

ROBERT BURNS

*E*ven after a week-long holiday, Saturday morning has a special feel. No one around us is bolting down a last cup of tea, keeping an eye on the clock tower. That fellow in the corner has been reading the newspaper for thirty minutes or more, slowly turning the pages.

Seated in the cozy breakfast room of the Murray Arms, we gaze out the window onto the High Street, watching the children of Gatehouse gambol about like four-day-old lambs beneath an azure sky.

Our waitress pauses at the table, a warm, maternal smile on her face. "That's ma wee Davie. In the red shirt." Though she's young, fine lines tug down the corners of her mouth and eyes. "His *da* is supposed to be watchin' him this mornin'."

No sooner has she spoken than a man her age with coppery hair and a muscular build saunters into view, hands shoved into the pockets of his tattered jeans. Davie, who's been wrestling good-naturedly with another lad, jumps up at once to greet his father. Adoration glows on the boy's face.

His mother looks away as she lifts our plates, but not before I catch the sheen of pride in her eyes. "Will ye be tourin' the area?"

"We're off to Cairnholy, hoping the weather holds."

"Aye." She's watching her family play on the cobblestones now. Saturdays may be relaxing for some of us, but she has a long day of work ahead. "BBC says we'll not have rain…" Her words trail off into a sigh, then she grips our plates more firmly. "Safe travels to you, then."

We finish the last of our tea, long grown cold, and leave her a generous tip before making our way down a zigzag hall toward the Ann Street entrance.

POETIC JUSTICE

Before we quit the Murray Arms, I turn to read the words neatly painted on the back of the steps leading to the next floor. On the highest step black lettering declares, "IN THIS INN IN JULY 1793." My editor will suggest that's too many in(n)s, but there it is. On the next step down is "ROBERT BURNS WROTE." Never mind all the *in*s; history was being made in the room to my left. And the last line reads, "SCOTS WHA HAE." My editor also might insist on a comma after "Scots," but I doubt Burns would mind. The song titled "Robert Bruce's March to Bannockburn" came to be identified by its stirring first words:

Scots, wha hae wi' Wallace bled,
Scots, wham Bruce has aften led,
Welcome to your gory bed,
    Or to Victorie!

This is the author at his most patriotic and impassioned; every stanza ends with an exclamation point. "Liberty! thou art a prize truly," he wrote in a letter accompanying the lyrics.[1] As we leave, I glance once more in the Burns Room, where the words were first put to paper although the poet arrived with the song already in his head. Can you picture him riding along, singing the phrases over and over lest he forget them? No wonder the lines have such a strong cadence, composed as they were on the back of a trotting horse!

We navigate the uneven cobblestones, climb into our mud-spattered car, and are soon heading southwest on a route parallel with the Water of Fleet. Tree-covered hills stand to our immediate right, and flat carse land lies to our left. The slow-moving Fleet travels in a straight channel, level with the grass; the land around it was drained for agricultural improvements two centuries ago. Brown sheep, and exceedingly woolly ones at that, graze near the banks.

One mile from Gatehouse a fifteenth-century tower house comes into view. Perched on a promontory, the stark gray walls of Cardoness loom over Fleet Bay. It's a steep climb to the castle, but the view is impressive. I'd be happy to stop, though we'll have a similar vista a few miles down the road when we visit Cairnholy, an ancient burial site high above the water.

You want to press on? Well and good.

While we still have Cardoness in sight, I'll tell you an *ugsome* story about the castle's final tenant. The McCullochs, proud possessors of Cardoness but poor financial managers, lost the property to their neighbors and archenemies, the Gordons. In a vengeful rage, Alexander McCulloch dragged the poor widow Gordon from her sickbed and threw her onto a dung heap, where he left her to die. Och, such a travesty!

His son, Godfrey McCulloch, followed in the violent footsteps of his father. In 1697 he marched upon the Gordon home with a loaded gun and fatally wounded his neighbor, William Gordon (who lived, ironically, in pious Samuel Rutherford's one-time house). Outlawed, McCulloch fled the country, then attempted a clandestine return several years later, taking up residence in Edinburgh. Brazenly attending a church service at Saint Giles, he was recognized by a Galloway man, who shouted, "*Steik* the door, there's a murderer in the Kirk!"[2]

Sir Godfrey McCulloch was arrested, tried, and sentenced to die on the Maiden. I saw this Scottish version of the guillotine in Edinburgh: a grisly piece of furniture. Legend says McCulloch was the last criminal to perish beneath its blade.

STONES ON A HILL

On a more pleasant note, isn't the weather splendid? Fair and sunny, but not eye-squintingly bright. We can't see the bay yet, but we're beginning to climb. That wee road goes to Anwoth Kirk; you'll remember we came out of the forest that way yesterday.

As the green hills on our right grow steeper, Skyreburn Bay appears on the left, and Fleet Bay beyond it, with a scattering of islands in the distance. If our day were clearer still, we might see the Isle of Man. Along the shoreline the ground's a bit boggy, with reeds poking up and a sign that cautions, "Danger: High Tide Channel." We'll be admiring the view from a safe distance.

Thomas Carlyle, the Scottish essayist and historian, was once asked by Queen Victoria to name the loveliest road in Britain. "The road from Creetown to Gatehouse of Fleet," he answered. Knowing he hailed from Dumfriesshire and was no doubt partial, she asked what the second loveliest road might be. "The road from Gatehouse of Fleet to Creetown."

Well said, sir. To this winding road along a broad expanse of water, add dark green woods, then wildflower meadows, then rounded hills, then craggy outcroppings of rock—an ever-changing scene. The bay reappears as we continue climbing. More hills on the right mean our exit for Cairnholy should be coming up.

Now let's see how your nerves are this morning. Before us rises a narrow, steep, tree-edged road with a precipitous drop and nowhere to turn if we meet a vehicle coming down. Would you prefer the crawl-along method or the pell-mell approach?

Right. Hang on. And try not to notice the blind curve near the top...

Yes! Another uneventful climb, my fourth to date. Five, if you count the highly eventful time I was almost mowed down by a lorry driver who'd also chosen pell-mell.

Fast or slow, the ascent is worth the effort. Welcome to the second or third millennium BC. Huge, jagged stones, thrust into the ground as if flung from heaven, surround a gaping burial chamber on the grassy summit.

Cairnholy is a breathtaking sight, bold in its starkness, cryptic in its design.

When my son and I pulled into this car park late one afternoon, he leaped out before we'd come to a full stop, so eager was he to explore the chambered cairns. He was soon photographing the mysterious array of stones framing a pale wintry sky and its transparent gibbous moon.

To have so sacred a place to ourselves, then and now, is a rare treat.

We ease through the turnstile and walk toward Cairnholy I, by far the larger of the two cairns. The empty chamber is fascinating enough, yet the eight tall pillars of rock, more narrow and angular than typical standing stones, are what give the scene an otherworldly appearance.

In any season and in any weather short of a downpour, the camera loves Cairnholy. From one angle the stones look dark and brooding; from another the white markings of the whinstone stand out like dabs of paint. I have photos of the stones drenched in mist, others with bright sun and shadow, still more taken at sunset with a pink-edged horizon. For perspective, I'll include a distant copse of trees or a flock of blackface sheep or the long gray line of a dry stane dyke.

To the north stands Cairnholy Hill, a broad, rounded backdrop. Wigtown Bay to our south is a wash of blue gray water. And on every side the land rises and falls in smooth, green waves. I can tell by the expression on your face *this* is the Scotland you've been waiting to see: ancient history and natural beauty, without a hint of the modern world.

For a few minutes the only sounds are the soft whir of our cameras and the bleating of sheep. Then from below us, the crunch of tires on gravel. We start toward the car park as another vehicle pulls beside ours.

A middle-aged man climbs out of a middle-aged Volvo. He'd thought fondly of 1973 when he dressed that morning. "Ladies!" he shouts, so brashly we wince. "Take a look at this place, will you?" The slam of his car door echoes throughout the peaceful glen.

I remind myself that the Lord loves everyone—even loud men in loud pants—and I'm called to do the same. "Cairnholy really is something," I agree, stepping aside so he can use the turnstile. "I hope you brought your camera."

"Nah." He flaps his hand through the air. "I just buy postcards."

FERRY THORN

Be thou a Bogle by the eerie side of an auld thorn…
Be thou a Kelpie, haunting the ford or ferry
in the starless night.

ROBERT BURNS

"Danger! Danger!" warn the signs along the mud flats of Wigtown Bay, a jarring note amid this scenic stretch of water and silken, mud-colored sand. We can assume such dire notices were not posted along the loveliest road in Britain when Thomas Carlyle admired it in the nineteenth century. The cautionary signs are primarily for visitors; natives know better than to set forth onto the solid-looking Wigtown Sands.

At high tide the water draws quite near the road along this east channel of the River Cree, as we see now. But at low tide the sands are exposed, and the far shore of Wigtown can look deceptively close. Over the years people have started across, certain they'll reach the other side—until the unthinkable happens. In his *Travels in Galloway,* Donald MacIntosh explains, "The tide can come in with quite astonishing speed, not just in a long, straight line towards you as civilized tides ought to do, but far off on the flanks where you cannot see it. Then after meeting behind you, it wraps itself around you cutting off all means of escape."[1]

Frighteningly visual, that description. I can almost feel the water crawling up my shins.

No doubt Wigtown Bay's shifting sands and unpredictable tides held enemies at bay—quite literally—for the former residents of Carsluith Castle, a tower house built along the coastal road in the early sixteenth century. Four stories tall, the ruins of Carsluith sit in the center of a newly gentrified retail establishment. The Carsluith Farm Shop and Tearoom, as well as the farm's stable of horses, look first-rate. We wave at a chestnut bay in passing, deciding to forgo this historic site as well. Strange how after only a week in Scotland we're nonchalantly thinking, "There goes another castle…"

The view truly is spectacular, with water stretching to the far horizon and misty blue hills in the distance. Ten miles farther along the A75 we reach the exit for Creetown. I bypassed this village my first few times around the bend, too eager to reach Loch Trool. But today we'll take a slight detour, seeking the legendary Ferry Thorn, a tree older than the village itself.

Auld Ferrytown of Cree

Turning right onto Saint John Street, we're soon in the heart of Creetown, not a cheery tourist town but a solid, residential village with gray and white houses lining the narrow streets. Parking on both sides forces drivers to take turns when other vehicles approach; the flick of headlights means, "You go first." Some cars are parked halfway onto the sidewalk, probably to spare their side mirrors getting clipped off.

Creetown's history is preserved in its street names: Harbour, Church, Bridge, Mill. The Barholm Arms is the old coaching inn, with the stables across the street. Farther up on the left stands the Ellangowan, a late-Victorian hotel named for an estate in Sir Walter Scott's novel *Guy Mannering*, set here in the parish of Kirkmabreck. Small though it may be—about 750 residents—the village boasts not only an attractive tower clock made of local granite but also a bowling green and two fine museums.

One is the Creetown Gem Rock Museum, which truly is a gem. The other is the Creetown Heritage Museum, there on the right—as it happens, not open most Saturdays—filled with vintage photographs of the village, historic artifacts, and memorabilia sufficient to justify the modest admission price. Three helpful museum volunteers—Val, Andrew, and John—were the kind souls who once directed me to Creetown's oldest living resident: a hawthorn tree, worth a short walk.

TREE LORE

After parking at a garage on the outskirts of town, we follow a well-trodden footpath through the long, emerald grass, flattened by wind. Despite clear skies, the air is raw and the breeze off the water, sharp; I'm glad for my jacket and watch you button yours up to your neck. The ground is slightly damp but not soggy as we tramp along a stone dyke in good repair, leading toward the broad burn, which empties into the Cree estuary.

In this flat, riverside setting of grass, water, and blackface sheep, the Ferry Thorn is impossible to miss: it's the only tree in sight, and it's been growing here for more than two centuries. Back in the day, the hawthorn served as a gathering place for travelers preparing to ferry across the four-mile estuary to Wigtown, summer or winter.

The first time I came looking for the Ferry Thorn, I was expecting a typical tree with broad branches sprouting from a straight trunk. Instead, I found a tall, gnarled specimen hanging over the stone dyke at a precipitous angle. Bowed by constant westerly winds off the bay, do you suppose? By sheer age? By soil erosion? Whatever the cause, the Ferry Thorn is bent but not broken. Even in mid-May, a few white blooms still decorate its leafy branches. By late September, bright red berries will have taken their place.

Mind the thorns. They're long and extremely sharp; women once used them for sewing needles. The old rhyme, "Creep under a thorn; it will save you from harm," suits this tree very well. Since the path continues beneath its low branches, creeping is advised.

You can be sure no one in Creetown will ever fell this tree, no matter how old or infirm it may become, and not just because of its historical significance or sentimental value. By longstanding tradition, hawthorns are sacred, a symbol of life and fertility. It is believed that cutting down a thorn invites grave misfortune.

Perhaps it's the isolated setting, the featureless landscape, the unnatural stillness, or just the strangely bent and twisted form of the Ferry Thorn, but we don't tarry in its presence. A dozen photos from all angles, a few shots of the sheep grazing near the stone embankment along the A75, and we're trotting back toward the garage at a good pace.

Rev. Dick called "the great mass of Cairnsmore" rising behind Creetown "very grand,"[2] dressed in a collage of colors in purple, brown, green, and tan. Cairnsmore of Fleet is even more stunning when viewed from the unnamed road that carries past the Gem Rock Museum. That northern route over the hills to Gatehouse of Fleet may be the loveliest stretch in Galloway. Would that we had two hours to cross the many bridges over the Moneypool Burn, to climb the endlessly curving path through forests and meadows, to look down into a deep, green valley and across the Cairnsmore, dipping down into Gatehouse only long enough to turn around at the Ship Inn and traverse the same road back, eager to see it all again from a different perspective. Especially in late August, when the mountain heather is bright purple and the bracken still green, when the sky is a shimmering blue and the sheep still graze on the braes, it's difficult to keep driving while blinking away tears.

Next time, dearie.

Less than a six-mile drive north, and we'll reach the old bridge that spans the River Cree, then aim for the glen of Loch Trool, another beautifully remote place where history and story meet.

INTO THE GLEN

If thro' that glen I gaed to thee,

My ain kind Dearie O.

ROBERT BURNS

*V*arious spellings can be found for the parish of Monigaff or Monygaffe or Munygaff or Moniegov or Minnigaff. That last appears on our O.S. map as the official version.

And the meaning? Two centuries ago Rev. John Maitland declared it meant "stony muir,"[1] and there are indeed many moors in this parish, the largest in Galloway. But Rev. Hugh Steele, the congenial former pastor of Monigaff Church, assured me it was pronounced "mini-gaff" if you made a small mistake and "moni-gaff" if you made several big ones. A dear fellow, Hugh is preaching in Annan now. On the Sabbath we'll see how the new man is getting on.

We're approaching Minnigaff on the B7079, which travels past a pretty meadow before reaching a grim stretch of council housing—government-subsidized apartment buildings—then carries us through the old settlement of Creebridge, which leads to (you guessed it) a bridge over the Cree. Let's quit short of crossing, though, and do a little exploring on foot.

Nice houses along this curve near the bridge, aye? Like that gray stone home with the wrought-iron fence tipped with gold fleurs-de-lis and a fringe of trees at the entrance. And what an exceptional view we have of the river. Swans glide along the surface, and fine old buildings and trees line both sides, with grassy verges leading to the stone-edged banks. Spanning the Cree is a handsome four-arched bridge in gray granite with tall black lampposts at each cutwater. Small, rounded projections give pedestrians a safe haven should cars approach from both directions, as they're doing now. That poor woman in the blue jumper stepped aside just in time.

Newton Stewart is across the way, a busy market town founded in the seventeenth century by William Stewart, the second Earl of Galloway; hence the name "New Town of Stewart." We'll cross the bridge and head south on Victoria Street in search of a bright red Royal Mail box for our postcards, but first, might I tempt you with a plate of fish and chips? Just behind us on the corner is the Cree Inn, a tidy, unassuming place nearly three centuries old. Made of whitewashed rubble, the two-story inn faces the bridge and has a one-story extension in the back, where we'll find lunch served. Lodging is no longer offered at the Cree, but pub meals are. Even before we open the door, the aroma of battered fish and fresh potatoes floats out to greet us. Posting our mail will have to wait.

PILGRIMAGE ALONG THE CREE

Our appetites sated and our postal duties attended to, we head north on the road I've been waiting all week to show you. Rev. Dick called this "one of the greatest journeys in Galloway."[2]

Since the road slowly ascends for ten miles over many a rolling hill, I'm not sure how he managed on his bicycle. Even in our car, it'll be slow going in some places. We *could* choose the well-paved A714 on the west side of the River Cree, but I've always favored the narrow yellow line on Landranger 77 that takes us through the wilds along the eastern banks.

Here's the entrance to Creebridge House Hotel, where we'll be lodging. After our trek through the rugged hills and glens, I think you'll find the civilized surroundings a welcome end to the day. For now, we've woodlands on our right and the Cree on our left. After a slight curve around the youth hostel, we take the bridge over Penkiln Burn, a dark ribbon of water rushing over unseen rocks and solidly flanked with trees. The moment our tires reach the far bank, we begin a steep climb past the old Monigaff Kirk, surrounded by a graveyard full of McKies—including several named John and more than a few named James—as well as a McBryde or two. The rubble ruins of the late medieval kirk stand proudly beside the newer sanctuary, built in 1834, where we'll worship tomorrow.

The road levels out as we curl around the church, then widens beyond a single lane, though not by much. Round black-and-white signs remind us of the thirty miles per hour speed limit. Beyond the hedgerows and stone dykes stretch untamed woodlands, cultivated fields, and meadows where flocks of glossy, blue black rooks poke about in search of food. Some properties bear signs—such as Knockman Wood—but most do not.

A mile along the way, where my fiction readers and I envision Penningham Hall, the Cree widens into a serene body of water once named Loch Cree, though it's no more than a broadening of the banks. River or loch, it's a lovely setting and heavily wooded. A canopy of trees, birch and oak among them, hangs over us as we move away from the water and cross an exceedingly narrow bridge.

We pass Drannandow Farm before we come to the Wood of Cree, a nature preserve, which the sign proclaims to be the "largest and best example of ancient woodland in southern Scotland." Otter, deer, and squirrels inhabit the wood; teal and mallard ducks live in its marshes; and redstarts and pied flycatchers can be heard—*hweet* for the redstart and a two-note *zee-it* for the black-and-white flycatcher.

And oh, the bluebells carpeting the forest floor! Even in heavy shade, their violet blue stalks are easily spotted from the road.

A half-dozen low, rocky burns have been diverted under our roadway, hastening toward the Cree from the hills through gorges carved deep into the ground by early spring thaws. With our windows open to enjoy the aromatic woods, we hear not only birdsong but also the sound of rushing water…and absolutely nothing else. Since we have yet to pass another car, I'm glad for your company on this isolated track.

Placenames like Low Cordorcan and High Camer Wood aptly describe the falling and rising terrain, as does Brigton, where we cross a wide bridge over the mingled Waters of Minnoch and Trool. We're nearing the Southern Upland Way, a coast-to-coast footpath across the Lowlands, covering 212 miles. *Challenging* is the word folk use to describe the route as it traverses varied landscapes like this one.

> Enormous gray boulders perched on the gorse-covered hillsides overlooking the road. Where old trees had toppled over in the boggy lowland, the exposed roots formed fantastic shapes, grotesque and marvelous at once.
>
> *Whence Came a Prince*

TURNING TOWARD TROOL

When we come to a T in the road, I'm disoriented, but only for an instant. To the left is a road leading to the A714; we'll take that easier route back to Minnigaff later. For now, we're headed northeast into the glen, a jewel among the Forestry Commission lands.

Even the endless plantation of conifer trees can't hide what's ahead. The massive hills don't bear the placename *ben,* meaning a mountain, but the granite range is still imposing. Buchan Hill is directly before us, dwarfed by the mighty Merrick to the north at 2,764 feet; as a point of interest, its nearest higher neighbor is on the Isle of Arran, a 2,867-foot peak named Goatfell.

Did I mention heights make me dizzy?

We've passed the Stroan Visitor Centre and are following the signs for Loch Trool. Already the hills are beginning to close in on us, much as they do in the Highlands. The rounded peaks are glacier-carved granite; the land has a wild, uncharted look. Our rough, narrow road feels like a logging track, as if we've taken a wrong turn, missed some main route. We've yet to see the loch, but it won't be much farther.

Less than two miles long, Trool can hardly compare in size to the two dozen miles of acclaimed Loch Ness, but it's a beauty. *Trool* comes from a variant of the Gaelic word *sruthail,* meaning "stream,"[3] which gives us a clue to how the loch will appear when we finally—

Ahhh.

She Walks These Hills

Th' outstretching lake, imbosomed 'mong the hills,
The eye with wonder and amazement fills.

Robert Burns

*F*orgive me if I sigh. The glen of Loch Trool almost defies description, though I'll do my best. Mysterious. Enchanting. Untouched. As if this were the one place on earth yet to be discovered.

Steep hills covered with heather unfurled before them,
forming a narrow glen with Trool at its heart. From this
vantage point, the water was a shimmering thread of
silver woven through the pines by a canny hand.

Whence Came a Prince

The loch bends slightly and broadens in the center; on that pine-sheltered elbow sits Glen Trool Lodge, built by one of the earls of Galloway for sporting ventures. If you've read my novels, you'll imagine this property as the McKies' granite mansion of Glentrool, nestled against the lower slopes of the Fell of Eschoncan. (I've heard various pronunciations, all of which sound like a sneeze.)

Eager to stretch your legs? That opportunity is literally around the bend. We're nearing the car park for Bruce's Stone, a monument to Robert the Bruce, who secured a stunning victory in 1307 against the army of Edward I by lining the summit of Mulldonoch with granite boulders, then rolling them down the steep slopes to crush the approaching English troops. Edward I—referred to as "Longshanks" while he lived and the "Hammer of the Scots" on his gravestone—died later that year. Though he succeeded in executing Sir William Wallace, Edward I failed to end Scotland's bid for independence, finally realized in 1314 at Bannockburn.

Bit of an uphill walk here along a craggy trail; at least there aren't any rocks headed in our direction. The temperature has dropped several degrees, and the breeze has stiffened. A posted sign declares the ascent of the Merrick "arduous"; hikers are further cautioned that weather conditions in the hills can deteriorate quickly.

I have no intention of climbing anything more challenging than this little mound of rock-encrusted grass and dirt with Bruce's Stone on top; just to be safe, I glance at the skies, hoping blue didn't turn to gray while we were busy admiring the glen. All is well above. And the ground beneath our feet isn't muddy or slick, I'm relieved to report.

At the top of the mound, we discover a couple of twentysomething athletic types perched on the other side of Bruce's Stone—one gazing through binoculars, the other snapping photos—both men outfitted for "arduous."

"Are you climbing the Merrick?" I ask, preparing to be impressed.

The brown-haired lad with the camera pauses long enough to say, "Aye," then goes on about his business. His companion, sporting a black ponytail tucked inside his insulated vest, barely glances over. Clearly, we won't be joining them, in our thin jackets and discount sneakers. Seconds later they bound down the sharp incline to the gravel path and strike out for the hills, leaving us to enjoy our miniature summit.

ALL FALL DOWN

Each direction we turn the view is beautiful. To the east, the mountains fold on top of one another, growing mistier and bluer with each distinct layer. South across the loch is the famed Mulldonoch. Tradition has it that Bruce stood on this side to watch the enemy's progress; at the opportune moment, three blasts of his bugle launched the boulders down Mulldonoch's precipitous sides. To the west is the most engaging panorama of the glen, with Loch Trool's contours outlined in pine green and the distant farmlands and hills painted in muted shades.

Bruce's Stone is a hefty rock, not unlike one of his weapons on that March morning. Most people scramble up here for the chance to look across the glen, not to read the plaque on the stone, however stirring the words: "In loyal remembrance of Robert the Bruce, King of Scots..." While you're composing your shots, I'll tell you a story of my last visit here, also in March, before most of the tourist sites were up and running for the season.

I had the glen all to myself that morning; even the Visitor Centre wasn't yet open. The weather was dry and mild, though it had rained the day before, and the ground was muddy in spots. I climbed up here without mishap, eager to use my going-away present from my husband: a brand-new Canon with a zoom lens and sleek design.

After photographing the glen of Loch Trool from every angle, I cautiously started back down the hill, letting the camera swing about my neck instead of doing the intelligent thing and tucking it in my pocket. Suddenly my foot slipped, and gravity took over. Down I went, tumbling over the sharp rocks, my brand-new camera leading the way.

"Help!" No one was around, of course, but you have to do *something* when you land in a broken heap. Even with my foot pinned under me, my camera worried me most, since mud and tiny stones covered the lens. "Help!"

Out of the blue appeared an older man with a shock of silvery hair and a sturdy build. "Och! What's happened here, lass? Have ye taken a tumble?"

I held up my Canon with a groan. "We both did."

He plucked the camera from my hands, deftly brushed off the last of the dirt, and examined the lens with a practiced eye. "A scratch or two on the case. Nothing to fret about." He made a minor adjustment, then handed the camera back to me. "Good as new."

That's when I noticed the professional-looking equipment draped around his neck. "Are you a…"

"Photographer," he said with a nod, then cupped my elbow to help me up. "Come, let's get you onto level ground."

Imagine, in that vast, empty glen, a man with camera know-how and strong arms showing up at the precise moment I was desperate for both. All I could say was, "Thank you, Lord." Which I did, about a zillion times.

That was day two of ten days in bonny Scotland. I hobbled every-where, but I managed—climbing steps, walking hills, and driving around Galloway—wincing all the way. When I arrived home and it *still* hurt, hubby sent me off to the doctor, who showed me an x-ray revealing a decidedly broken foot.

"See these two bones?"

I squinted at the x-ray. "I count three."

"Precisely." He snapped off the light box, a stern look on his face. "You'll have to stay off it for eight weeks, Liz. In a cast. No standing, no walking, no driving."

Did this man not understand the job requirements of motherhood? "I'll have you know this broken foot has fifteen hundred Scottish miles on it." With that I stood, walked out of the office, and drove home.

Honestly, it only hurts on rainy days. And on Edinburgh cobblestones.

Goujons and Hot Pots

Glen Trool Lodge may not be open to the public, but we're staying at another one of the Earl of Galloway's properties. After a more direct, though still scenic, drive south on the A714, we're settled in for the night at the Creebridge House Hotel, built for the earl in 1760 amid three acres of gardens and woodlands at the foot of Kirroughtree Forest. The stone exterior isn't a solid gray but a pleasing mix of natural grays and browns, brightened by white trim and a row of dormer windows, with peaked roofs like a row of carets from your keyboard: ^ ^ ^ ^ ^.

We're staying in a twin-bedded guest room at the far end of a long hall with an intriguing three-steps-up, four-steps-down passageway. Travelers used to modern hotels might find it a nuisance; one guidebook called it "a maze inside."[1] We, of course, find the meandering hallways charming. The room faces east, overlooking the gardens—a promising prospect for the morning.

True to the earl's sporting interests, guests may choose from a dizzying array of activities: salmon fishing, golfing on a course mere steps away, taking nature walks, mountain biking, pony trekking, bird watching. As for me, I'm tempted to curl up with a book in front of the crackling log fire, a welcome touch this cool May evening. We're in the hotel's drawing room, a seventeenth-century abbreviation for withdrawing room, where guests are received. Though it's spacious, the oversized furniture and dark woods make for a cozy setting.

"Mrs. Higgs, what may we serve you for dinner?" An efficient-looking young woman stands before us, hands folded behind her back, no order pad in sight. I know a pro when I see one. And isn't this a brilliant way of doing things? We lounge about in comfy upholstered armchairs while our meal is prepared, then are escorted to the table in tandem with our food. Much nicer than sitting in a straight-backed chair playing with our silverware and eating stale crackers.

Our walk in the glen has made us both ravenous; judging by the menu, we've come to the right place. Just reading the list of starters makes my mouth water. I'm having the Criffel rarebit toasted on french bread with caramelized shallots and a crab apple with mint chutney. You're trying the terrine of duck, pigeon, and Highland venison, served with a warm black currant and blueberry compote and Arran oatcakes. (On Arran, restaurants serve Galloway oatcakes.)

"Have you decided on your main course?"

We have indeed, and both contain delicious-sounding ingredients. But the names are a bit of a puzzle. Do I take a stab at the pronunciation, adding a French flair? Or simply point to the menu?

I'm going for it. "I'll have the *goujons* of chicken breast."

Our waitress doesn't laugh, but I do when I'm served deep-fried chicken strips. Who knew? Be warned: if you order goujon in America, you'll be staring at a plate of flathead catfish. Your menu selection is easier to pronounce but harder to visualize: lamb hot pot. Aren't most cooking pots hot? Or is it *served* in a pot?

Once we're seated at our cloth-draped table in the Garden Restaurant, with its two-tone ivory walls, blond hardwood floors, and french doors opening into the landscaped gardens, our questions are answered and our taste buds rewarded. My sole regret is not ordering steak, if only to taste the special sauce made of whisky, forest mushrooms, and thyme. Maybe I could sing that one to our waitress to the tune of "Parsley, Sage, Rosemary, and Thyme."

Then again, she might offer me a free spoonful if I promise not to.

AULD KIRK, NEW KIRK

From scenes like these, old Scotia's grandeur springs,

That makes her lov'd at home, rever'd abroad.

ROBERT BURNS

*W*eren't we just here, seated in the gold and white Garden Restaurant? Except now Sunday morning sunlight is streaming through the french doors, and we've pots of tea and racks of toast scattered around us. At a corner table a harried mother spreads strawberry jam on toast for her impatient brood and wags her knife like a disapproving finger. "Your da will be here any minute," she scolds, as the children continue to paint their faces with jam.

This is the embarrassing truth about traveling: if you're not careful, you spend most of your waking hours deciding where to eat, what to eat, and when to eat again. To avoid that problem, I'll often have a hearty late breakfast, then enjoy dinner as early as possible, with nothing in between except tea and a biscuit, saving both money and time. But that's when I travel alone and would rather research history than study a menu. With a traveling companion, chatting over meals is part of the fun.

Shall we walk to church since the weather is fine?

A quick stop at the reception desk to settle our bill, and we're out the door, greeted by riotous birdsong, dappled sunshine, and a slight breeze. This may be our warmest day yet. I expect the temperature to reach sixty; sorry, fifteen Celsius. Since we're on foot, we'll skip the long driveway and take the shortcut down this sloping path leading to the sidewalk. Clever, the way it's built into the garden wall.

With the service starting at ten, we can take our time and see a bit more of the village. Drinking in the lilac-scented air, we walk the length of the main thoroughfare, stopping short of taking the bridge across to Newton Stewart. Instead we snap pictures of the old tollhouse, shaped like an octagon cut in half and attached to the far end of the bridge. A cozy-looking *biggin* and rich with history, the small building once sheltered the person charged with collecting the bridge toll. In recent years it's housed a shop, a counseling center, and a classroom. The sign above the door reads "Ye Olde Toll Bar," though the place looks deserted.

Strolling north on Creebridge Road, we're flanked by white, gray, and brown houses from the past two centuries. One natural stone home notes "1769" above the door in a flowing script, and the shoemaker's house is dated 1772. No two homes are exactly the same, yet all share a simplicity I've come to love, free of garishly painted shutters or cunning door hangings or modern brass fixtures. Whatever keeps our Scottish friends from adding those decorative (but historically inaccurate) touches, they have my heartfelt thanks.

Following the sidewalk around the high garden wall of the Creebridge House Hotel, we're now on Millcroft Road, where the houses stand apart from one another and hence have larger gardens. Most are set back from the road, with driveways and landscaping and stone dykes and all manner of suburban touches, though we've walked only a short distance from the bridge. Glorious annuals in vibrant pinks, soft lavenders, and bright yellows line the driveway of an old home partially hidden by greenery.

At this very curve in the road, I had a most unusual experience one September afternoon. A petite, elderly woman with large glasses and striking white hair was walking toward me, requiring one of us to step off the narrow sidewalk. I did so at once, in deference to her age, then murmured a greeting as we passed each other.

She spun around and said without preamble, "There's an American who writes Scottish fiction and lives in Wigtownshire. A lovely Christian woman. Have you met her?"

Taken aback, all I managed was, "Um…not yet."

"You must ring her up," she insisted and told me the author's name, assuring me she'd be listed in the British Telecom directory.

Indeed, she was. When I related the story by phone, my newly found writing sister laughed and said, "That could only be Lily Murphy." A local legend apparently.

But we never sorted out how Lily knew who *I* was. My photo doesn't appear on my book covers, and I seldom introduce myself as an author unless I'm approaching someone for an interview. However small the villages of Galloway are, they're not *that* small. Might a heavenly nudge have sent Lily in my direction?

As cars whoosh by, you and I continue single file, talking and pointing as we go. That pretty stone guesthouse with the walled garden is Flowerbank, which young Edgar Allan Poe visited in the summer of 1815. Interesting how the residence faces the garden rather than the road, like the mansions in colonial Charleston, allowing the breeze off the water to cool the house; in this case, I suspect the initial owner merely wanted to enjoy a view of the River Cree. The four-story corn mill in that cul-de-sac has been recently restored and converted to apartments—*flats* here.

Two low painted signs mark Old Edinburgh Road off to the right—little more than a path running through the moors and hills—and Old Minnigaff, beginning with this cluster of eighteenth-century houses. We bear west at Maple Cottage and climb over the bridge, slowing our steps to enjoy the gentle sound of flowing water.

My camera seems to have leaped out of my purse and into my hands. Who can resist with scenery like this? As we start up the hill, which feels far steeper on foot, the centuries-old belfry comes into view between the branches of an overhanging tree.

> The medieval kirk stood high above the watery confluence of the Cree and the Penkill, overlooking their union like a minister presiding at a wedding ceremony. The rising mist from the river and burn swirled round the headstones—the oldest in Galloway, parishioners boasted.
>
> *Whence Came a Prince*

You know what I'm going to ask of you. Truly, it's a splendid kirkyard, and the gravestones are particularly old, and the shade trees magnificent, and…

Bless you, dearie. Lunch in New Galloway this afternoon. My treat.

LIVING STONES

We tiptoe into the kirkyard, silent except for the rushing waters along the eastern edge. On the far side of the new kirk, churchgoers are filing inside, chatting and laughing as they go; here among the graves, all is quiet.

I shiver, though the air is still, and gaze at the remains of the auld kirk: a long rectangle made of whinstone; two pointed windows of late medieval styling; facing east, a graceful arched doorway, still intact; the birdcage belfry, high and lifted up. And buried on every side are parishioners long gone to their reward. "Believe and look with triumph on the tomb," one epitaph boldly proclaims.

Surrounded by trees and draped with ivy, the gray rubble ruins of the

old parish kirk stand as a testimony to humankind's enduring faith in God. Why else would these stones still be here, century after century, when they might have been carted off to build houses or dykes or bridges?

It seems these walls were raised for a holy purpose. "Ascribe to the LORD the glory due his name; worship the LORD in the splendor of his holiness."[1] His glory still shines here; the sunlight pouring through the leaves, illuminating the scene, reminds us of that truth. And his holiness remains as well; we sense the mystery of his presence.

A woman behind us clears her throat. "Worship's aboot to begin."

As we turn to acknowledge her, she smiles and gestures toward the berry red doors. Nodding our thanks, we follow her across the spongy grass, admiring the present church with its buttresses and stained-glass windows and square tower, finished the year before Queen Victoria's coronation: the new kirk.

SURPRISED BY JOY

Inside, organ music floats down from the balcony, which is mounted on three of the four painted walls. No box pews are in sight, only rows of dark wooden pews, which match the wainscoting in the front of the sanctuary.

Even after the *beadle* dutifully carries the Bible up the pulpit stairs, the lofty pulpit stands empty. We soon find out why: the pastor is working the room, welcoming people and shaking hands. His bald head tips back whenever he laughs, which is often. Rather than a robe, he's wearing a gray suit, blue shirt, and gold tie. Even those look too restrained for his enthusiastic demeanor. I can't guess how old he is. Sixty going on thirty by the look of him.

Locating an empty pew, we join the hundred or so worshipers, who seem happy to be there. Again no printed program, though we don't miss it. *Surprise us.*

Pegging us as visitors straight off, the woman beside me whispers loudly, "Pete and his wife came to us from Zimbabwe."

"Really?" I peer at the minister more closely. "He looks Scottish."

"Oo aye!" She chuckles, blue eyes twinkling. "Pete was once a millionaire as well." When my mouth drops open, she continues, "He gave away his business in South Africa to do the Lord's work, then felt called to return to Scotland."

Are you thinking what I'm thinking? *Go, sell your possessions.... Then come, follow me.*[2] Whatever this Pete fellow has to say, he certainly has my attention.

The service begins promptly at 10:00 on an upbeat note, with the congregation singing from a modern hymn book, *Mission Praise,* rather than using a hymnary. Even so, just words, no notes. The assembled are, for the most part, middle aged and elderly, though younger faces beam among the crowd, including a handful of children.

"What happens next?" I ask as we sit down.

"Och, ye ken." She shrugs, smiling. "A hymn and a thing and a hymn and a thing."

We sing each hymn with gusto, not worried about being too loud, and watch the service unfold. An impromptu testimony is shared, announcements attended to, scriptures read by parishioners, and intercessory prayers lifted up. A woman named Jenny leads several youth in a sidesplitting drama about Jonah, communicating a meaningful lesson amid the laughter. During the offering, the upright piano is pressed into service, with violin and oboe accompaniment. Touched by the music, we're glad to add our pound notes to the offering bag as it slips by.

When it's time for his sermon, Pete remains on the floor of the church, preaching from notes that can't be more than an outline, so extemporaneous is his style. He's a preacher more than a teacher, admonishing and encouraging as he moves about, Bible in hand, pacing the floor, adjusting his glasses, adding enough humor to keep us engaged without distracting from his message on forgiveness, both timely and timeless.

How his church must have loved him in South Africa! Clearly, he is appreciated here. I've been to many a Church of Scotland service, but I must say, none quite like this one at Monigaff. An hour later we stand in line to say a quick word to the pastor, knowing he has a second morning service at Kirkmabreck Church, where the parishioners of Creetown await.

Pete warmly shakes our hands. Before we can speak, he says, "You must be the Americans."

I'm dumbfounded. Is it how we dress? How we sing?

He beams at us both. "I believe you've already met our Lily."

Indeed I have. When a smiling woman with big glasses and a bigger smile steps forward, I clasp her tiny hand in mine. "I've been longing to know what compelled you to approach me on the street that day."

"The Holy Spirit told me to," she says simply, giving me a squeeze. "We're to speak to strangers, you know. Some people have entertained angels without knowing it."

I'm hardly an angel; as for Lily Murphy, I can't think of a better description.

WILD AND WOOLLY

Admiring Nature in her wildest grace,
These northern scenes with weary feet I trace.

ROBERT BURNS

*P*repare yourself: it's time to go wild…and woolly.

Yesterday's adventure into the glen enclosed us in woods, meadows, and valleys; this afternoon's journey will be high and windswept, remote and often barren. And hilly? That's not the half of it.

The woolly part is, I confess, more sheep—black face, white face, mottled face, and woollier than ever with shearing season approaching.

Having walked back to our car at Creebridge, we depart Muny-Monie-Minnigaff with fond memories tucked in our hearts and head northeast on the curve-laden A712. This part of our route is called the Queen's Way in honor of Elizabeth II. Steep hills rise and fall around us as we travel through the Galloway Forest Park on an ever-winding road carved into the hillside. For sixteen miles the only turnoffs are cycle trails and forest tracks, which I doubt the car-hire company would approve our taking. True, there is at least one tarred road off to the left, but it leads back into town.

Rev. Dick pegged this road: "where one sees no living creatures but sheep and moor-fowl."[1] Even on this blue-sky Sabbath, we've not seen more than a few vehicles. That's Cairnsmore of Fleet again to our east, a gently rounded but significant hill, rising 2,331 feet. Novice climbers take note: this one's for us, with a plainly marked path, a steady but not strenuous ascent, and amazing views from the summit.

Admittedly, the view so far has been neither wild nor wind-swept. The picnic table at Glen of the Bar with a family unpacking their luncheon hamper is a decidedly tame sight, but Highland-like vistas are ahead. We continue weaving through heavily forested hills, conifers crowding both sides of the road, until a break in the greenery reveals Palnure Burn on our right and Murray's Monument rising high on our left.

The obelisk isn't unique, but Alexander Murray surely was: an eighteenth-century shepherd who taught himself Latin, Hebrew, Greek, French, German, Welsh, and Abyssinian before beginning his formal education at the urging of Robert Burns. Murray was only thirty-seven when Edinburgh University named him Professor of Oriental Languages. Alas, his health failed, and he died the same year. Scotland has not forgotten Murray or his linguistic accomplishments. His birthplace, Dunkitterick Cottage, is a bit farther along.

Grey Mare's Tail is the name of that wee *linn,* not to be confused with the two-hundred-foot waterfall of the same name between Moffat and

Selkirk. This pretty stream of water cascades down from Grey Mare's Tail Burn, splashing onto the rocky ground below.

GET YOUR GOAT

And now a car park, which truly is wild because of what we'll find there: wild goats. A good number of sightseers have already gathered, and another car is pulling in behind us. No matter; plenty of room, plenty of goats. Grab your camera and take a look.

> Brown-and-white goats perched on craggy shelves no
> wider than their hooves. Their staccato bleating sounded
> as if they were laughing. *Ha-ha-ha-ha-ha-ha.*
> *Thorn in My Heart*

A stout wire fence at the base of Craigdews keeps the wild goats from leaping onto the roadway and onlookers from traipsing into their territory. The gray and white ones are my favorite, each with different markings.

Several goats wander toward us, apparently unafraid of their two-legged visitors. Kids are everywhere, on both sides of the fence: human kids hang on to their mothers' hands, eyes wide in wonder, and goat kids stand beside their mothers, noses up, ears alert.

"Look at him go!" a blond-haired boy cries, pointing to a goat bounding up the rocky hillside, which sets the other children in motion like toppled bowling pins as they point and shout. The adults exchange smiles and shake their heads when the goats take off, startled by the high-pitched squeals. Not all wild creatures have fur.

When we pull back onto the A712, following the path of the Palnure Burn, we're struck anew by the sense of isolation in this wilderness. Were we among fellow travelers minutes ago? And singing in a church not long before that? Neither seems possible, immersed in these lonesome hills, studded with gigantic boulders. I half expect an antlered buck or Pictish warrior to leap from behind them at any moment.

Four miles farther a green Forestry Commission sign on our right invites us to explore Raiders Road, an old drovers' track featured in the S. R. Crockett novel *The Raiders*. I paid the toll and drove it once: ten long miles of bumpy, unpaved forest road along the banks of the Black Water of Dee. Though we might indeed spot deer, otters, or ravens, let's press on to the Visitor Centre on the banks of Clatteringshaws Loch, a man-made reservoir of stunning proportions.

CLATTERING SHAWS

The name means "noisy banks," from a time when the Black Water of Dee flowed through this barren landscape, tumbling over glaciated rocks.

After the dam was built in 1929, a portion of Old Edinburgh Road disappeared beneath its waters, along with a bridge that our fictional Jamie McKie crossed one dark October night.

> Before him stretched nothing but moors, desolate and
> uninhabited, rife with bottomless mossy patches that
> could swallow man and beast in one black, gurgling
> gulp.
>
> *Thorn in My Heart*

In a moment we'll see peat moss up close. What astounds the eye just now is the seemingly endless loch mirroring the bright sky. And the blue green hills, long and gently sloped, surrounding the water. The dam is sizable too—at 1,562 feet, the largest in the Galloway Hydro Electric Scheme. (In the U.K., a "scheme" is a good thing, not a nefarious plan. Unless, of course, you once owned a cottage that's now at the bottom of the loch.)

Two things might interest you here at the Visitor Centre: a reconstruction of an Iron Age roundhouse and another Bruce's Stone. Same man, same enemy, same year, but a different battle in a different place; hence, a different stone.

We follow the marked path to the timber roundhouse, a family residence, rather like a Native American tepee. Here the thick sticks are placed horizontally instead of vertically, attached to poles radiating from the pointed top to the wide, round base mounted on stones. Fascinating to duck inside. The broad gaps between the sticks suggest they were once covered with thatch.

Emerging from the shadowy interior back into the afternoon sun, we continue along the path to Bruce's Stone on Raploch Moss. Here comes the wind-swept part: a broad, flat sea of peat, traversed by a boardwalk just wide enough for one person. I glance down at the grayish brown peat and wonder how boggy it might be. Would I sink if I stepped into it? And how far exactly? To my ankles? My knees? The boards beneath us give with each step, like some moving sidewalks in airports do—an uncomfortable sensation.

Finally we reach the huge commemorative rock where Robert the Bruce is reported to have rested after defeating the English yet again. The actual site of the battle is not far to the southwest, submerged beneath Clatteringshaws Loch.

A few photos, and we're relieved to be heading back across the boardwalk. Desolate would be a kind description for this place. Even so, a young couple approaches, staring at the flat marshland with wrinkled brows.

"I'm telling you, that's what the guidebook says." He brandishes a tattered copy. "Close to the Loch is Bruce's Stone," he reads aloud. "This overlooks the place where, in 1307, a small group of Scots defeated a force of English soldiers by starting a landslide which buried them."[2] He slaps the book against his thigh. "How can you start a landslide with peat moss?"

We glance at each other. Shall we put him out of his misery?

"Sir, there's another Bruce's Stone west of here in Glen Trool."

"Oh." He frowns at his guidebook. "Is there enough elevation there for rocks to tumble down?"

"Definitely." I laugh in concert with you. "And tourists as well."

An Afternoon
of Villages

The village-bell has told the hour,
O what can stay my lovely maid?

Robert Burns

*F*or six roller-coaster miles I've resisted saying, as I always do, "Our next stop is one of my very favorites." New Galloway *is* a charming burgh, especially after driving across stark, uninhabited hills with names like Gallows Knowe and wondering if we've seen the last of civilization.

Here we have sheep on the braes and a farm in the glen and a tall spire in view and the prospect of lunch—aye, my treat—and another High Street to explore. Welcome to New Galloway, dearie.

The village isn't the least bit new, of course. It's been a royal burgh since 1630, despite initial protests from rival market town Kirkcudbright, nineteen miles south. Such economic concerns were unfounded. Due to its remote setting, New Galloway claims but three hundred residents—the smallest royal burgh in Scotland.

Hard to imagine the community once hosted four annual fairs. Today's visitors are quieter. Anglers come with fishing gear, hoping to catch pike, trout, perch, or salmon in Loch Ken, while birdwatchers are on the lookout for willow tits in the damp woods and great crested grebes floating on the loch, necks drawn back and bills tucked in.

On my frequent visits to New Galloway, I have one stop in mind: The Smithy, down at the bottom of the High Street next to a sweet, flowing burn. A guest or two can find lodging in the original blacksmith's shop, but it's lunch we're after. We'll park near the phone box in case you want to make a quick call home, then to The Smithy we go.

Flowerpots blooming with bright peonies and pine tables in the front courtyard invite alfresco dining on sunlit summer days. When we push open the front door, we're greeted by a shopful of gifts and then by the owner, a congenial fellow with a balding pate and a delicious pâté on his menu.

"Plenty to look at," he says, waving a hand over the display tables and shelves as if sprinkling them with fairy dust. "Take your time."

I've seldom left this place without making a purchase, if only because the selections are so unusual, including carved walking sticks, handmade leather purses, and picnic backpacks. I once found a pair of embroidered pillow covers stitched to look like rows of old books. How long do you suppose I hesitated over *that* purchase? Another time I unearthed a gorgeous set of Pimpernel hardboard placemats—the Antique Roses pattern—*on sale.* (They weighed a ton in my suitcase, but that's why the thing has wheels.)

The Smithy's book section not only boasts Scottish history, regional wildlife, and interesting biographies but also fiction classics: Stevenson, Buchan, Munro, Rutherford, Scott. Since I've already purchased my jar of lemon curd for this trip, I'll keep my hands off the marmalades, preserves, and chutneys, but I make no such promise about the jewelry.

After a bit of judicious shopping, we follow our host into the adjoining dining room with its warm ivory walls and sunny bank of windows. Windsor chairs are pulled up to round wooden tables with fruit-patterned vinyl cloths, and a glass-fronted dessert case tempts us as we pass.

Was that an apple tart?

Choosing a table by the window, where various plants fill the broad sill, we're soon studying the menus. I can't help noticing how clean they are; my fastidious father made us leave restaurants before ordering if the menus were soiled or grease stained. (As a child, I was mortified; as a mother, I'm thinking it's not a bad idea.) No need to flee The Smithy, where everything is fresh, nothing is fried, and the air is scented with fruit and cinnamon.

That *was* a tart, wasn't it?

And look what they serve: haggis. Not yet? Smoked venison, perhaps. No? Well, you can't go wrong with a plate of Lockerbie cheese, and I'll have an egg mayonnaise on granary, or whole-grain, bread. Notice how they offer children's portions and grannies' portions. Such a winsome word, instead of seniors. (If you wore granny glasses in 1966, you're old enough to qualify for the smaller portion, grandchildren or not.)

Our host returns almost at once with tea. "What brings ye back to New Galloway?"

This is when you know you've visited a tad too often. I smile in your direction. "My friend wanted to spend ten days in bonny Scotland."

"Where've ye been, then?" He nods in approval, smoothing a hand over his neatly trimmed beard as we describe our itinerary. "Aye, those are the best bits."

In a few minutes he's back with our plates. Twenty minutes later dessert arrives: a treacle scone for you, and for me...well...you know. Served warm. With Cream o' Galloway ice cream.

The Village with the Very Long Name

You'll not mind a quick drive along the High Street before we head north? We could walk, of course, but we've a good deal more ground to cover and haven't seen the last of the wild and woolly landscape.

That's the Water of Ken down there, sparkling in the afternoon sun. A mile south, below the ruins of Kenmure Castle, the river spreads into Loch Ken, then eventually turns into the River Dee, which empties into Kirkcudbright Bay. Are you starting to visualize a map in your head? (If not, that's why Benny drew one for us at the front of this book.) We're about to come full circle on our trip; this evening we'll pass Thornhill en route to our lodging.

Interesting, isn't it, how more residential cottages than shops line the High Street? The Kenmure Arms is the old coaching inn. Most Scottish villages of any size have one; what amazes me is that they're still standing and doing a lively hotel trade as well. Several B&Bs flank the High Street too. No wonder *holidaymakers* come here, with such lovely views across the Ken.

The white and gray mid-Victorian town hall, with its large, square clock tower and steep pyramid roof, is impressive for a burgh this size. Since the population has remained steady over the last century, we can only assume New Galloway has always done things in style.

Time to find somewhere to turn around. Roomy side streets and driveways aren't common in older villages. Watch behind us for traffic, will you?

We wave at The Smithy in passing, then turn onto the A712, resuming our eastward journey. The graceful Ken Bridge with its five arches, built in the early 1820s, carries us over swift-moving water. Now the difficult decision: continue on the A712 and climb up, up, up to Balmaclellan, which offers an incomparable view of a prominent range of hills known as the Rhinns of Kells? Or turn north on the A713 and take a gander at the village that so inspired Rev. Dick he admitted, "I could not hope to rise to the lyrical eloquence that it deserves."[1] Since you really can't go wrong in this beguiling corner of the world, let's follow our bicycling minister north and find out why the next village is so extraordinary—other than its long name.

We're traveling along the serpentine Water of Ken, the eastern hills pressing us close to the riverbanks and the Holm of Dalry, a low, flat spot in this otherwise hilly terrain. The holm is full of grazing sheep, and the mountains in the distance are a smoky blue.

Without much notice, here's our second village of the afternoon: Saint John's Town of Dalry. When the Knights of Saint John of Jerusalem, who once owned this land, founded the town, they called it Saint John's Clachan, meaning a hamlet or village; hence, the Clachan Inn by the roadside. Though the locals call their home Dalry, from the Gaelic *dal righ* or "king's field,"[2] there's a place in Ayrshire with that name too, which must drive the Royal Mail folks batty.

My notes about Dalry say "hilly, curvy, pretty"; it's definitely all three. Just look at the flower beds in the garden of that peach-colored B&B! We'll park across from the Lochinvar Hotel, another coaching inn from the mid-eighteenth century, much updated during Victoria's reign and covered with Virginia creeper ivy. One bright autumn day when I came through Dalry, the entire front of the hotel flamed a brilliant dark red, like fire captured on a leaf. I was so stunned I stopped in the middle of the street and snapped a photo; silly me for not parking here in front of the old stables.

Just ahead at the northwestern point of this triangular village is Dalry Parish Church. We approach and push open the black metal gates, admiring the long avenue of lime trees that shade the drive, with their gnarled trunks and bright green leaves. A fragment of the old church (1546) stands near the new one (1832). Its gray whinstone and white painted dressings are quite beautiful, as is the pastoral setting, with the church on a rise overlooking the churchyard. And there's a mote—how did I miss that last time?—another pudding-shaped earthwork that's been quietly sitting there for centuries.

Only when we retrace our steps do we notice the stile at the entrance, a graceful curve of ascending stones meant to carry visitors over the wall when the gates are locked. We're soon out on Main Street, climbing the long, steep block to the heart of the village, where the Clachan Inn and the Bank of Scotland claim two corners and a fine old fountain stands in the middle of the street like a mercat cross of old. The houses here are trimmed in distinctive, even bold, colors. Deep purple. Snappy blue.

Bright-as-sunshine yellow. Flowers festoon every cottage, whether hanging, climbing, or growing in a tiny front garden. No wonder Rev. Dick found Saint John's Town of Dalry charming.

Back in our car, we head up Main to Kirkland Street, the third leg of this triangle and the oldest road through Dalry, trod by many pilgrims—including James IV—en route to Whithorn, site of the hallowed shrine of Saint Ninian, the first Christian in Scotland. An accounting kept by the Lord High Treasurer on a pilgrimage in 1497 indicates small sums given to the priest at "Sanct Johnis Kirk of Dalrye."[3] The antiquity of the town shows as we descend narrow Kirkland past a row of old cottages, every one painted and trimmed in white with a black door.

If I could, I'd snap a picture of that black-and-white cat curled up on the windowsill. Do you suppose he was in on the paint scheme too? I seldom see felines here, except in bookshops. I can only presume that when dogs took over Britain, all the cats sailed to France.

We drive the other two legs of our triangle once more, then continue northeast. Once again the last cottage ushers in the first sheep, and we're climbing up the A702, heading toward Thornhill. Fasten your seat belt, and grab that handle above the window; it's wild hills and bleak moors for the next twenty miles. The map gives us fair warning, listing almost no properties yet tons of hills—some with curious names like Milnmark, Barscobe, and Troquhain, and others that are more easily understood, such as Hog, Ewe, and Brown.

At the moment, we have a wide open vista, though the peaks ahead promise otherwise. A slender finger sign points to the footpath leading to Holy Linn Waterfall, where seventeenth-century Covenanters, forced from their churches, baptized children in the cascading water.

Rather than gently rolling slopes like we saw near the Solway, these rougher, treeless mounds wrestled their way out of the earth—a shoulder here, a knee there—knocking the road for a loop. Occasional color appears in the form of bushy yellow gorse or vivid orange poppies or straight stalks of yellow broom, softening the rugged wilderness the same way blooming cacti do in the American West.

Squeezed between Stroan and Blackcraig Hills, each about 1,300 feet, we long for a straight, even road, if only to settle our stomachs. My heart's still in the Lowlands, but the rest of me seems to have taken a Highland detour. *Oof.*

Third Time's the Charm

Though the trees end abruptly, the rolling terrain does not; crazy, undulating hills force the stone dykes to rise and tumble with them. Soon the scenery is greening up again, the shadows begin to lengthen, and we've reclaimed Landranger 78 from the backseat. We're approaching our third village of the day: one with a short name that's a *tickler* to pronounce. How would you say *Moniaive*? (Hint: in 1790, the minister of the parish spelled it Minniehive.)

If the word for Dalry is hilly, the word for Moniaive is narrow. Picturesque, historic, charming, and several other words also suit this burgh of barony, included in *The Most Beautiful Villages of Scotland*.[4] After following the Castlefairn Water for several miles, we arrive in Moniaive and are immediately thrust into a traffic situation, with three roads converging at the mercat cross.

The main route through Moniaive is not only narrow but also curvy.

And where did all these cars come from? Images fly by as I grip the wheel: one-story cottages with colorful trim; windowpanes with swirls in the center; a row of thick, black poles, like hitching posts; a grocer selling Cream o' Galloway; the familiar red sign for the post office. We're almost at the bridge. Is that a parking space in front of the George Hotel?

When I pull over without using my turn signal, the man behind us in the Fiat doesn't honk, though he does frown loudly as he drives by. Considering the George Hotel is one of the oldest inns in Scotland—1624— I think it deserves a quick look.

It's easy to imagine horses being led across the street to the old stables or devout Covenanters, persecuted for their opposition to the episcopacy of the church under Charles II, taking refuge in a hiding place halfway up the stair. Once inside the green and white inn, we let our eyes adjust, then survey the interior: original flagstone floors, old wooden lintels over the windows, exposed beams overhead.

A woman in her fifties appears. Judging by her apron, she's doing double duty in the kitchen. "Is it lodgin' ye're after? Or supper?" She's frowning, but not loudly.

"Neither," I confess. "We just wanted to…see the George."

"Aye, aye." She rests her hands on her hips. "Suit yerself."

She stands there, guarding the premises, while we quickly inspect the fireplace with its small square hole where extra coins were once left by the George's patrons so men of the road—tramps, if you will—could have a meal. Now the money is given to charity. There's a handful of quid in there. When the frowning woman isn't looking, we add a few more.

Murmuring our thanks, we head back out into the sunshine to find our car wasn't so much parked in a space as abandoned by the roadside. On a quiet Sunday, no one seems to mind.

The A702 takes us over the bridge, at which point we're immediately forced to choose between going straight or turning right, with both roads leading to Penpont. Geographically impossible? Not in Scotland. Right seems to be the best choice, heading east from the village and along the Cairn Water through a peaceful valley where the railway once ran. A few more miles and we're home for the night—our last in Dumfries and Galloway.

BANKS O' THE NITH

The Thames flows proudly to the sea...
But sweeter flows the Nith to me.

ROBERT BURNS

*J*ust west of Thornhill on Penpont Road, the Nith Bridge, with its two stone arches, was nearing completion in April 1776 when the middle pillar gave way. According to the tersely worded public records, the builder's error "made it absolutely necessary to take down the whole work and rebuild it again."[1]

Notice I'm mentioning this *after* we've safely driven across the one-lane bridge.

All at once we're enveloped in woodlands and presented with a dilemma. Two roads led from Moniaive to Penpont, but three roads lead from Penpont east to Thornhill, each pointing in a different direction:

north, east, and south. Since we know where we're headed, we confidently turn right on the B731, skirting Thornhill on a pretty, wooded road that leads us directly to the A76.

The land is refreshingly flat after our up-and-down escapades over the A702, though hills are never far away; those are the Lowther Hills to the northeast and the smaller Keir Hills to our immediate west. After turning onto the road leading to Trigony House, we still can't see the hotel, surrounded as it is by four acres of gardens and woodland: the perfect setting for an Edwardian shooting lodge.

Trigony House was built by the owners of nearby Closeburn Castle, one of the oldest continuously inhabited castles in Scotland. The rectangular keep, with its iron yett still in place, dates from the fourteenth century and the mansion house attached to it from the nineteenth century. Can you imagine living in a place with a crenelated parapet and a vaulted prison in the basement?

If you're a Kirkpatrick (or Kilpatrick), then your ancestral roots are planted here. Sir Roger Kirkpatrick of Closeburn Castle was a fierce advocate of Scottish independence. During the Wallace campaigns, his motto was "Touch and I Pierce." (Ouch.) And when Robert the Bruce stabbed the Red Comyn at Greyfriars Church in Dumfries (we stood in that spot a week ago), the Bruce was not alone. Tradition holds that Sir Roger administered the fatal wound; hence, the family crest features a hand holding a bloody dagger.

Well, on to more pleasant topics, like this lovely red sandstone lodging house with its tall, slender windows and thick drape of ivy across the front. As we park the car, we see that the front door is slightly ajar, inviting us inside.

Above the entrance, carved in stone, we're welcomed with the words

"The Lord bless thy going out and thy coming in." Inside we find rich paneling along an open staircase, a low fireplace tucked beneath the stair, leaded glass windows on the adjoining wall, and a bit of whimsy by way of a wooden rocking horse named Trigony.

And here comes Jan to greet us—smiling loudly, I might add.

A tall young woman with medium-length blond hair and a kind face, she consults the reservation book, tapping it with her pencil. "Superior twin with a garden view. Right this way, if you please."

We're escorted to a spacious room in a back corner of the house, decorated in browns and golds with a long bank of casement windows that do indeed face the garden. Like every other window I've seen in Scotland, these have no screens. A wide window seat provides space to crank open the windows and enjoy the circle of flower beds below.

After pointing out the various features of the room, Jan presents us with our key, a genuine one made not of flat plastic but of brass, as all of them have been on this trip. Keys that fit into keyholes and hang from an engraved wooden tag or a braided tassel. *Real* keys that feel good in your hand.

Pausing at the door, she reminds us, "See you in the lounge at 7:30."

Can it be that another three-course dinner awaits us and a Full Scottish Breakfast twelve hours later? Good thing we're on a ten-day tour. Twenty days, and we'd have to buy new clothes for the trip home. In a bigger size.

A Burns Refrain

Rev. Holland, you'll recall, described the various kinds of precipitation in Scotland. Last on his list was one he deemed "a nuisance," and that's *smirr.*

Often used in a phrase—a smirr o' rain—it's akin to another Scots word, *smuir*, which means "a dense, enveloping cloud of mist."[2] You can't exactly see smirr, but you can feel it.

> A light rain hung in the air, so fine it did not fall so
> much as rise, like mist. *Smirr*, Duncan called it.
> Overnight the temperature had dropped, leaving a
> numbing chill that seeped into his bones.
> *Whence Came a Prince*

The temperature *did* fall overnight; I closed the casement window just before dawn, having awakened shivering in my narrow bed. Steaming bowls of porridge and more tea than usual warmed us at breakfast, and the heater in the car kept our feet toasty on our short drive south, past Friars Carse to our first stop of the day.

We're walking toward the steading of Ellisland now, a tidy, white-washed farm on the banks of the Nith. Robert Burns took possession of Ellisland in 1788 at Whitsuntide—this particular week in May, as it happens. *Did he have smirr as well?* I wonder. The fine rain certainly casts a drizzly pall over the scene, though only for those who labor outdoors. Sitting by a cozy fire with a cup of tea

while looking out at the mist rising from the River Nith is my idea of a perfect morning.

We stop at the ticket desk, and I discover my membership cards are of no use at this privately owned museum.

"Sorry, mem." A gentleman who might qualify for the granny portion patiently waits while I fish out my coin purse.

When I find sufficient pounds for us both, I slip them into his hand with a wink, letting him know we're happy to oblige. Support historic preservation? Absolutely. "I believe Mr. Burns paid an annual rent of fifty pounds. Does that mean if we visit ten more times, we could rent Ellisland for a year?"

"Och!" The word dissolves into a wheezy chuckle. "Ye'll not want to miss the film." He points toward the granary, a small, separate building among the many facing the cobblestone courtyard. Inside we find a stack of chairs and one long, wooden church pew facing a screen.

Two women sit at the far end of the bench, speaking softly in German. A small family—father, mother, preschool boy—are perched on the other end, as if prepared to bolt unless the film starts soon. An older fellow sits alone in one of the chairs, staring at the blank screen. Quite a crowd for a Monday morning. Was it the dreich weather that brought them all out? Did they think this was the bank holiday instead of next Monday?

We settle in as the lights fade to black and Ellisland appears on the screen, bathed in sunlight rather than smirr. While the narrator introduces us to the farm's most famous tenant, I'm taking mental notes—my only option. I can hardly whisper into my tape recorder, and it's too dark to write anything. When the film ends sixteen minutes later, the German women wander off toward the Nith, the older fellow stays put—maybe he's hoping for a second feature—and Mom and Dad are practically running toward the car park, whiny Junior in tow.

Our self-guided tour of the steading includes a look in the stone *byre* where Burns's Ayrshire dairy cows would have been sheltered and at the ploughs and scythes on display. When the two women from Deutschland fall in step with us, I try to remember a simple greeting from my college semester of German.

"Guten Dach," I say brightly, but they wrinkle their brows. Haven't I just said, "Good day"?

"Guten Tag!" the younger of the two says, suddenly grinning. "You said, 'Good roof.'"

So much for my foreign language skills. *"Ja."* I smile back at her, pointing up at the blue gray slates brought from Lancashire long ago. "Guten Dach."

With German-American diplomacy restored, we step inside the plain farm cottage: one story, built of rubble, and furnished for the time period. Walking about, grateful to be dry, we picture the newly wed Jean Armour working at her stove built into the kitchen hearth and her husband bent over his books. Encased in glass are his wooden flute and a few small books, a precious commodity then, costing as much as a horse.

Even if this isn't the actual building where Burns wrote—that cottage was torn down and replaced with this one in the early nineteenth century—the room was designed with a writer in mind. The desk is fitted into a corner, with pastoral views from two low windows, and a small fireplace on the right would keep fingers from growing stiff in the cold. Once again the desk steals my attention. The front leaf drops down to create a writing surface, revealing a row of little drawers atop tall slots, where papers could be neatly stored.

Whether because of his writing pursuits, his excise duties, or the stubbornness of Ellisland's soil, Burns failed as farmer and moved his family to Dumfries in 1791. Yet he always thought fondly of this stretch of the Nith—"That winding stream I love so dear!"—and undoubtedly left a bit of his heart on its bonny banks.

We walk out to the farm steading, where the dykes have been rebuilt many times yet still contain some of the stones Burns collected from river and field. Though the air remains cool and damp, the smirr has ceased, and the gray sky has lightened enough to give us hope. As long as the spongy grass won't swallow our feet, we've ideal weather for tromping around Dumfriesshire's most secluded castle.

Wrapped in Green

We've not far to go; just north on the A76 for ten or eleven miles, and we'll be there.

Well, *almost* there. Morton Castle is hidden from view, with no signposts from the main road to point the way. Simply finding Morton is part of the thrill; when you see the setting, I think you'll agree it's worth the effort.

First we'll backtrack a bit, passing through Auldgirth, Closeburn, and Thornhill, slowing to thirty miles per hour through each village. After so many days of new places and new experiences, it's comforting to see something familiar. At Carronbridge, we veer right onto the A702, headed toward Durisdeer. You're thinking we're retracing our steps from last Sunday morning? Not completely, my friend. Long before we reach that road, we'll take a different one.

When it comes to locating Morton Castle, guidebooks are little help, saying things like "northeast of Thornhill, on minor roads east of A76." Yes, but *which* minor roads?

Here's how I found the one we're going to take. See that sign pointing downhill to the left: "Drumlanrig Castle: 4 Miles"? I figured two castles surely would have a road connecting them. And so, several Mays ago, I did what we're about to do: take the unmarked road to the right, head up the steep hill, and beg for divine guidance.

Hedgerows line both sides. Very tall, very thick, very not-see-through hedgerows. The road is so narrow I fear for our side mirrors. If another vehicle comes barreling around that turn, we're toast. We keep inching along, praying we have the road to ourselves, searching for any indication we're going the right direction.

When another road crosses ours, I trust my instincts and keep going uphill. We pass a farm called Morton Mains, which is encouraging, but the castle is a Historic Scotland property. Surely there was a sign we missed…

Aha! No more than a finger of wood, painted forest green with white lettering, but still a sign: "Morton Castle."

The road deteriorates to a muddy track, and woods hover over our right shoulders, but we're there. We choose the driest-looking spot to park the car and climb out, gazing with wonder at our hidden treasure.

No one is here. No one, it seems, has ever been here.

Across a velvety, barren rise looms a circular tower attached to a lofty

wall, which disappears behind a lone pair of trees. In the winter, when the branches are bare, another tower is visible. The ground encircling the castle drops precipitously into a sylvan loch. With the Lowther Hills in the distance, the effect is one of bright green on deep green on rich green on dark green. In the shadow of those hills are pastures; we can hear the sheep bleating, so faintly as to seem imagined.

We open the broad gate, then wince at the sound when we latch it behind us, as if we might disturb something or someone. The silence is eerie, the wind capricious, the view indescribable: like a golf course on a mountaintop. Drumlanrig Castle, far below us, looks inconsequential indeed.

Other castles have come and gone from this scene of desolate beauty, dismantled or burned by war. By the early eighteenth century, the site was abandoned, if not forgotten.

After taking countless photos, we climb the steps that lead into the ruins. A dungeonlike hole in the corner brings to mind the tragic tale—

more legend than history, I suspect—of one Lady Morton, who gave her heart to a young manservant. When the earl learned of their illicit affair, he threw the young man into the dungeon. Undaunted, Lady Morton visited her beloved in secret, bringing him food. Alas, when the Earl of Morton discovered their duplicity, he strapped the hapless young man to two unbroken colts and released them into the wilds of Dumfriesshire.

Our gray, melancholy sky fits the story. The mist has lifted, but the clouds have not; the sun is nowhere to be seen. Midday is upon us, and the drive north toward Glasgow beckons. I can't think of a better last view of Dumfries and Galloway than this one. For the moment, we'll take Rev. Dick's advice: "One is prone to linger for a while before crossing the Nith and realizing that all is at an end!"[3]

LOOKING NORTH

Mark the winds, and mark the skies...
Round and round the seasons go.

ROBERT BURNS

*W*ould you like to see Durisdeer once more, that lovely old church where we worshiped last Sunday? I see. Better to hold our memories close than try to re-create them.

We'll turn our car in the other direction then and aim for Sanquhar. Far beyond it waits Lochwinnoch, only minutes from the airport. (Sorry, didn't mean to mention that word.)

Since we took our headlong plunge down the narrow road from Morton Castle, the sky is quite altered. Dove gray has softened to pale blue, and the clouds have been pulled apart like cotton candy, stretched into long wisps.

I ease off the gas pedal as we near the entrance for Drumlanrig Castle. Truly, if you want to stop, it's a magnificent property... Well, perhaps you're right. Morton Castle, remote and mysterious, was the perfect coda to our trip.

Known as the "Pink Palace," Drumlanrig is everything that Morton is not: a painstakingly maintained seventeenth-century estate belonging to the Duke of Buccleuch and his family, with priceless artwork and furnishings on display throughout their opulent home. Alas, when four men in a white Volkswagen stole Leonardo da Vinci's *Madonna with the Yarnwinder* right off the palace walls, the estate ramped up its security efforts, allowing guided tours only. The days of wandering unescorted through the palace and tarrying on the grounds with the peacocks have sadly come to an end.

Nonetheless, isn't our fresh perspective of the countryside grand? This time we're driving toward the Lowther Hills instead of away from them and ascending rather than descending. We've not left the Nith behind just yet and won't until we reach New Cumnock; for the next twenty miles or so this broad ribbon of water will keep us company.

And here's the sun, no longer encumbered by clouds, shining its soft, angled light across the Nith Valley, turning the fields into green and golden splendor. So lovely, this rural scene. Though I know the twenty-first century has put down roots in Dumfries and Galloway, the eighteenth century—and the fourteenth and the tenth—are well planted here too. When I'm home, I read about Scottish history, but when I'm here, I can grasp it with both hands.

Have you come to love the Lowlands as I do? Perhaps you're already making a list of possibilities for your next visit. Caerlaverock Castle, along the Solway coast southeast of Dumfries, is more accessible than Morton yet just as inspiring. You might press on a few more miles and discover the eighth-century Ruthwell Cross, housed behind the pulpit of Ruthwell Parish Church, where the intricately carved Anglican cross rises seventeen feet from a sunken apse.

In Wigtownshire, Glenluce Abbey is almost as ethereal as Dundrennan, and the Castle Kennedy Gardens and Logan Botanic Garden make for a fine green-thumb outing. For a walk on the wild side, follow the treacherous path to Dunskey Castle, perched on a barren sea cliff near Portpatrick with "Danger!" signs posted everywhere. Thrilling.

As to the month you might return, though May in Scotland is unquestionably beautiful, October is—dare I say this?—equally stunning. Oh, the colors! And the mist on the moors, and the cry of a golden plover echoing across the silent hills. Autumn visits yield the best photos: not sunny and bright, but gray and misty. Photos that actually look like Scotland instead of like postcards. While we're heading northwest, trying to pretend our trip isn't almost over, may I describe for you an October day in the Lowlands?

Dawn approaches more slowly and arrives with damp feet. Mist, fog, even frost may cling to the ground and coat your windshield. Sometimes the mist is alive, swirling and crawling over the land, and other times it's as still as a sleeping cat. The skies are more pewter than blue in October, yet startling days of vivid brightness often send people wandering outdoors to gaze at the firmament.

Because the sun is warm but not hot, anglers, hikers, golfers, bicyclists, and hunters make the most of the fine weather. Scottish children have a fortnight break from school in October, meaning the castles and abbeys ring with young voices. Amateur photographers like us have a field day—quite literally—when autumn rolls around. The distant hills are a dusky blue, the mist and the light conspiring to turn them into a mirage.

> The rising mist softened the bright colors of the oak
> leaves, creating a muted blend of burnt orange, golden
> yellow, and pale brown.
>
> *Fair Is the Rose*

Muted is the word. Every conceivable shade of green, gray, brown, yellow, orange, rust, and red is painted across the landscape, with a touch of black pigment lowering its intensity but never its beauty. According to my diaries, in mid-October the trees are at that lovely transitional stage: half covered with the green leaves of summer, the other half surrendering to autumn, draping each tree with color, like fringe on a shawl.

Oaks and maples appear to be posing for a postcard, holding their branches just so, waiting to hear the click of a shutter, hoping no one will notice that the grass is as green as ever. January? Same green. July? Same green. Aye, it's a brighter, iridescent green in May, but the grass is unmistakably green year-round.

Silver birches, with their small golden leaves, draw one's gaze along river and wood. Beneath the trees, thickets of bracken—large ferns that can reach shoulder height—contain every color in the same cluster of plants: light green, yellowish tan, ruddy beige, dark brown.

The light is even more slanted in October, with the sun rising to about ten o'clock in the sky, skirting the trees but never rising much higher. Near the Solway, flocks of sea gulls, white with black on their wings, swoop overhead as farmers plow their fields before colder weather and shorter days settle in. From the first of the month to the last, the stretch from sunrise to sunset is reduced by two full hours.

Perhaps driven by the same sense of urgency, roses make their last bid for attention, blooming all month and into November: old garden roses in creamy white, soft pink, buttery yellow, dusky red—all velvety and fragrant.

> The mild climate of east Galloway meant that even
> now, well into autumn, a few blooms remained. Leana
> carefully lifted one fading Damask rose to her face and
> sank into its silken center, inhaling the sweet perfume.
>
> *Thorn in My Heart*

So you see, October in the Lowlands is an excellent option. And that's only five months from now. A consoling thought.

You've only sighed once, passing the tearoom in Sanquhar, where you tasted your first sausage roll and tried milk in your tea. As for me, I watched Dumfries and Galloway in my rearview mirror until the last hill disappeared from view.

Even the best holidays must end, dear one. I do hope you'll be pleased with our last stop.

FINAL RESTING PLACE

Of all the kind things my husband has ever offered to do, this is my favorite: I asked him to hire a piper to play at my funeral should I enter the Promised Land before he does. With an earnest expression, he said, "Would you like me to take your ashes to Scotland and sprinkle them over Galloway?"

I didn't know whether to laugh or cry, so I hugged him instead. The man knows me well. Or maybe he was simply arranging in advance for a solo trip abroad…

Ah, here's the last road we need today: the A760. Under two bridges, our innkeeper, Janet, said, then on the left, behind tall trees. East Lochhead Country House is what we're after.

Good for you, spotting it before I did. *Barr* is the operative word in this neighborhood: Barr Castle, which we passed a moment ago, and Barr Loch, which we'll be able to see from our room. The farmhouse is only a century old—och! listen to me—and sympathetically restored.

Quite an establishment, East Lochhead. Self-catering cottages around the courtyard and a regular working farm with black Hebridean ewes and brown-spotted Jacob sheep. And dogs, of course. If there were cats, I'm afraid they've already left for Marseille.

Here comes Ross to greet us; no doubt he heard the dogs barking as we drove up. Animal friendly, this family, and keen on the environment.

"Here you are, then!" He has a jovial manner, with the white hair and rosy cheeks to go with it; like Santa, if Mrs. Claus put him on a strict health regimen. "Not far to drive today?"

I glance at my watch. *Oops.* We've arrived before we were expected. How gracious of him not to mention it. "We need to pack this evening," I explained. "Our flight in the morning…"

"Aye, aye, 9:00. Best be there by 7:00."

He doesn't know me; we'll be at the Glasgow airport by 6:30. We've already made our final petrol stop, thrown out stray shopping bags, and collected our O.S. maps from the floor of the car. One by one, I'm checking off my mental list of must-dos. The hardest to manage will be the last: *leave Scotland.* If I think of it as *fly home,* I'll do better.

With help from Ross, we cart our bags up the stair to a room overlooking Barr Loch. Interesting they don't call it Loch Barr. Local custom, I imagine.

It's a spacious room, tastefully decorated: an antique wardrobe with an arched door, a pretty dressing table in front of the window, and pristine white bedspreads. Gazing out at the rolling landscape, I find it hard to picture the airport being just fifteen minutes away. We'll be glad for that proximity when the alarm goes off at sunrise.

"Dinner is served at 7:00," he says and leaves us to our task.

All those purchases we stuffed in the boot are now spread out over two beds. Two dozen books didn't seem like that many last Wednesday. Was my pottery bowl always that size? I fear your antique birdcage is bigger. At least our jewelry will fit.

This is when I bring out my secret weapon.

At the bottom of my suitcase, buried beneath wrinkled clothes and spare shoes, nestles a zippered carpetbag. "Ta-da!" I hold it up, enjoying the look on your face. "This is how we get it all home."

Lined with our sweaters—we'll hardly need them when we get off the plane—the flexible carpetbag swallows all our breakable items with room to spare and plenty of cushion, leaving space in the two suitcases for books and birdcages and such. Dutiful U.S. citizen that I am, I've tallied all my purchases, proud of myself for staying under the duty-free allowance and keeping the receipts to prove it.

We reward ourselves with a relaxing walk in the garden, which wraps around two sides of the house. How Janet finds time to keep it looking so well tended, I can't fathom. I recognize a few of her flowers: star-shaped columbine with deep violet petals, and cranesbill in pink and lavender. When we move inside for dinner, we can still see the garden as the shadows lengthen across the lawn.

JUST DESSERTS

The aroma of roasted lamb mingles with the smoky scent of a log fire, a delightful combination. The table is set for two; it seems the other B&B guests won't be joining us for dinner. "Leg o' lamb, just for you," Janet says agreeably. She shares her husband's coloring: gleaming white hair, pink skin, and bright blue eyes. Made for each other, they were; the two met at a cricket match in the Yorkshire Dales.

When dessert is served, I grin; it's the one thing you haven't tasted but wanted to.

"Have you had cranachan before?" Janet asks.

"I have," I admit, smiling at the tall, frosty glass placed before me. "It's looovely."

"Older folk call it cream crowdie." She gives us long spoons. "Toasted oatmeal whisked with double cream, castor sugar, and a few drops of vanilla."

I savor each spoonful, hardly missing the raspberries some cooks toss in.

"They used to serve cranachan at farmhouses on festive occasions." Her smile has a tender look to it. "This being your last night in Scotland, I thought you might want to celebrate."

"Aye," I say, swallowing hard.

HASTE YE BACK

Fare-thee-weel, thou first and fairest!
Fare-thee-weel, thou best and dearest!

ROBERT BURNS

I'm holding *Highways and Byways in Galloway and Carrick* in my hands like a lifeline as the flight attendant pulls the door snugly closed and locks the handle in place. I can see her from where we're seated in 24D and F, the window and aisle seats. A small but welcome blessing: no one claimed the center seat, giving us room to fold up the armrests and stretch out a bit.

I always think I'll sleep on the way home, but I never do.

There's nothing to see out the window just now but luggage trucks. Nothing that looks like Scotland except the sky, which has three distinct bands of color: pale blue, silvery gray, and milky white. By nightfall it may rain. Or it may not. I sigh, remembering we won't be here to find out.

Eyes closed, you've tucked one of the airline's napkin-thin blankets under your chin. Sleep well, my friend. I open Rev. Dick's book to the last chapter, curious to see how he concludes things. Farewells, endings, stopping points are difficult for me.

It seems they were hard for him as well: "I am sorry that in beginning this final chapter I cannot promise the reader a grand climax."[1]

That's it exactly. Unlike fiction, where both story and protagonist have defined arcs that start and finish and soar in the middle, real life simply continues. Little rises and falls occur, the occasional dramatic shift, but otherwise each day is a steady unfolding of the lives we're called to live.

I sink against the window as the plane pushes back. We're first in line on the runway, so there's no delay; wheels turn and engines roar, preparing for takeoff. Seated behind the wings, I can almost feel the jet straining to leave the earth.

At last we're airborne. The emerald green hills of Renfrewshire come into view as we bank right and begin our long journey across the pond.

I blink, lest I miss my last look at Scotland, then realize you're leaning over my shoulder, watching too.

A WEE WORD

Some books are lies
frae end to end.

ROBERT BURNS

*N*ovelists don't think in terms of lies but rather of truths rearranged to suit the story.

In *My Heart's in the Lowlands,* every place described is as real as real can be. I've been writing this book in my mind for many seasons, giving the well of my heart time to fill: travel diaries from nine visits to Galloway, more than two thousand photographs, and a dizzying number of books about Scotland (eight hundred or so, but who's counting?). From those resources I spun a journey for us, then returned to Dumfries and Galloway just before this book went to press, making sure every detail was correct.

Of course, life goes on. B&Bs, shops, and restaurants change hands or close their doors, so by the time you read this, some facts will no longer hold true. Should you visit Scotland and discover a discrepancy here and there, please forgive me. And do let me know; I'm always honored to hear from readers.

As for the people who joined us on this journey, some are real and some are…well, characters. Actually, they're *all* characters, but some live and breathe in Scotland, and others live only in my imagination. In the foreword of *Five Red Herrings,* Dorothy Sayers explains, "All the places are real places…and all the landscapes are correct." Then she admits, "None of the people are in the least like the real people…. All that is just put in for fun."[1]

Quite right.

Of the people who surface throughout these pages, the following can be counted among Scotland's 5.1 million residents: Rev. James Scott; Angus Fordyce; Rev. Bill Holland and his wife, Helen; Benny Gillies and his spouse, Lyn, phoning in her appearance; Jo Gallant; Rev. Hugh Steele; Rev. Pete Aiken; Lily Murphy; Jan Moore; and Ross and Janet Anderson. The other folk we've met along the way are a composite of the many interesting people I've encountered in my travels. As my publisher would have me say, some of the characters and events in this book are fictional, and any resemblance to actual persons or events is coincidental.

One real person who appears regularly without a proper introduction is artist Simon Dawdry. An honors graduate of the Glasgow School of Art, Simon created original sketches of four dozen favorite landmarks in Dumfries and Galloway. Well done, lad.

You'll find a wealth of up-to-date information about Scotland waiting at www.LizCurtisHiggs.com: colorful photos taken throughout our ten days in bonny Scotland; favorite Celtic music CDs and where to order them; a host of recipes, including treacle scones, oatcakes, bridies, cranachan, and, yes, sticky toffee pudding; suggested B&Bs, restaurants, and more places to visit; links to helpful Scottish Web sites; and recommended reading for travelers, armchair or otherwise.

A note about spellings: modern topographical names differ from those in common use during the periods in which my novels are set. Newabbey is now New Abbey, Dalbeaty has become Dalbeattie, Penkill Burn is more properly Penkiln Burn, and so on. The contemporary spellings I've used in this book are widely accepted and appear on the O.S. maps. One bit of trivia: Glenelg is the only seven-letter palindrome in Highland topography.

In closing, I'm indebted to many kind Scots: antiquarian bookseller Benny Gillies, for serving once again as my on-site editor and cartographer; Janette Tait, owner of one of the liveliest Christian bookshops in Scotland, for her informative e-mails; Rev. James Scott of Durisdeer, for being so exceedingly helpful on the phone and even more generous in person, walking me about the churchyard and sharing his parish's history; Angus Fordyce of Cavens Country House Hotel, for a warm welcome and splendid meals; Rev. Norman Hutcheson of Urr, for helping me sort out the Irish yews and sharing details of his parish's quadricentennial celebration; Rev. Bill Holland of New Abbey and dear Helen, for opening their home and hearts to me many times; Steve and Christine Laycock, formerly of the Douglas House B&B, with manifold blessings on your new venture in Kirkcudbright; the personnel of the Selkirk Arms and the Murray Arms Hotels; Les Byers, curator of Ellisland Farm; Stephen and Sarah Donnan of the Creebridge House Hotel; Adam and Jan Moore of Trigony House

Hotel; Ross and Janet Anderson of East Lochhead Country House and Cottages; and Rev. Peter Aiken of Monigaff, for the delightful phone chat and the greater joy of hearing him preach.

Also a wee word of appreciation to Lorna at Edinburgh Tartan Weaving Mill and Catriona at Edinburgh Castle, who both assured me that people may now freely dress in the tartan of their choice.

My deepest thanks go to my talented (and patient) editorial team: Sara Fortenberry, Dudley Delffs, Jeanette Thomason, Laura Barker, Carol Bartley, Matthew Higgs (son or not, he was paid for his efforts!), and especially my brilliant husband, Bill, who looks for typos, offers encouragement, and sends me off to Scotland again and again with his generous blessing. I can never thank you enough, sweet man. For everything.

Before I bid you farewell, my friend, if you'd enjoy receiving my free newsletter, *The Graceful Heart*, printed and mailed just once a year, or would like an autographed bookplate for any of my books you kindly own, please contact me by post:

Liz Curtis Higgs

P.O. Box 43577

Louisville, KY 40253-0577

Or visit my Web site:

www.LizCurtisHiggs.com

Until we meet again, on one side of the pond or the other, you are a *blissin*!

Notes

First Light

1. Charles Hill Dick, *Highways and Byways in Galloway and Carrick* (London: MacMillan & Co., 1916), 43.
2. Dick, *Highways and Byways,* 112.

Heading South

1. Gilbert Summers, *Fodor's Exploring Scotland,* 6th ed. (New York: Fodor's Travel Publications, 2005), 103.

To Kirk We Go

1. Charles Hill Dick, *Highways and Byways in Galloway and Carrick* (London: MacMillan & Co., 1916), xiii.
2. Brian Fraser, *Churches to Visit in Scotland* (Edinburgh: Saint Andrew Press, 2000), 95.
3. Matthew 18:20.
4. John Sinclair, *The Statistical Account of Scotland 1791–1799,* vol. 4, *Dumfriesshire* (Wakefield, England: EP Publishing, 1983), 154.
5. Fraser, *Churches to Visit in Scotland,* 95.
6. Dorothy Wordsworth, *Recollections of a Tour Made in Scotland in 1803* (1894; repr., Edinburgh: James Thin, 1974), 11.
7. Genesis 5:24.

Country and Town

1. John Wesley, quoted in Dumfries Town Centre Partnership, *Dumfries Time Traveller* (Dumfries: Dumfries & Galloway Libraries, 2000), 31.

Homeward Bound

1. Mairi Robinson, ed., *Concise Scots Dictionary* (Edinburgh: Polygon, 1985), 514.

2. Herbert Maxwell, *The Place Names of Galloway* (1930; repr., Dalbeattie, Scotland: Castlepoint Press, 2001), 94.

3. Brian Conduit, *Dumfries and Galloway Walks* (Whitefriars, Norwich, England: Jarrold Publishing and Ordnance Survey, 1997), 72.

4. Charles Hill Dick, *Highways and Byways in Galloway and Carrick* (London: MacMillan & Co., 1916), 30.

A Sense of Place

1. John Sinclair, *The Statistical Account of Scotland,* vol. 5, *Stewartry of Kirkcudbright and Wigtownshire* (Wakefield, England: EP Publishing, 1983), 287.

2. Charles Hill Dick, *Highways and Byways in Galloway and Carrick* (London: MacMillan & Co., 1916), 32.

Holy Ground

1. Betty Willsher, *Scottish Epitaphs* (Edinburgh: Canongate Books, 1996), 39.

2. John Sinclair, *The Statistical Account of Scotland,* vol. 5, *Stewartry of Kirkcudbright and Wigtownshire* (Wakefield, England: EP Publishing, 1983), 182.

History Lesson

1. Theodore Roosevelt, quoted in Evan Thomas, *John Paul Jones* (New York: Simon & Schuster, 2003), 4.

2. John Sinclair, *The Statistical Account of Scotland,* vol. 5, *Stewartry of Kirkcudbright and Wigtownshire* (Wakefield, England: EP Publishing, 1983), 185.

3. John Mactaggart, *Scottish Gallovidian Encyclopedia* (1824; repr., Perthshire, Scotland: Clunie Press, 1981), 373–74.

Burgh of Barony

1. Charles Hill Dick, *Highways and Byways in Galloway and Carrick* (London: MacMillan & Co., 1916), 495.

Sunlight and Shadow

1. Charles Hill Dick, *Highways and Byways in Galloway and Carrick* (London: MacMillan & Co., 1916), 499.

A Misty Afternoon

1. John Gifford, *The Buildings of Scotland: Dumfries & Galloway* (London: Penguin Books, 1996), 353.

Of Smugglers and Monks

1. S. R. Crockett, *Raiderland: All About Grey Galloway* (London: Hodder & Stoughton, 1904), 139.

New in Town

1. Charles Hill Dick, *Highways and Byways in Galloway and Carrick* (London: MacMillan & Co., 1916), 85.
2. Harry Lauder, quoted in Angela Cran and James Robertson, *Dictionary of Scottish Quotations* (Edinburgh: Mainstream Publishing, 1996), 192.

Making History

1. Dorothy L. Sayers, *Five Red Herrings* (1931; repr., London: Hodder & Stoughton, 1984), 7.

Over the Hill

1. John Gifford, *The Buildings of Scotland: Dumfries & Galloway* (London: Penguin Books, 1996), 373.
2. Herbert Maxwell, *The Place Names of Galloway* (1903; repr., Dalbeattie: Castlepoint Press, 2001), 9.

Fair Anwoth

1. John Sinclair, *The Statistical Account of Scotland,* vol. 5, *Stewartry of Kirkcudbright and Wigtownshire* (Wakefield, England: EP Publishing, 1983), 136.
2. Hugh Palmer, *The Most Beautiful Villages of Scotland* (London: Thames & Hudson, 2004), 44.
3. John Gifford, *The Buildings of Scotland: Dumfries & Galloway* (London: Penguin Books, 1996), 315.
4. Dorothy L. Sayers, *Five Red Herrings* (1931; repr., London: Hodder & Stoughton, 1984), 5.

Castle and Cairn

1. Robert Burns, *The Complete Poetical Works of Burns,* Cambridge Edition (Boston: Houghton Mifflin, 1897), 286.
2. Thomas Bigging, *A Nook in Galloway* (Gatehouse of Fleet, Scotland: J. R. & A. Kirkpatrick, 1911), 26.

Ferry Thorn

1. Donald MacIntosh, *Travels in Galloway* (Glasgow: Neil Wilson Publishing, 1999), 50.
2. Charles Hill Dick, *Highways and Byways in Galloway and Carrick* (London: MacMillan & Co., 1916), 151.

Into the Glen

1. John Maitland, quoted in Sir John Sinclair, *The Statistical Account of Scotland*, vol. 5, *Stewartry of Kirkcudbright and Wigtownshire* (Wakefield, England: EP Publishing, 1983), 269.

2. Charles Hill Dick, *Highways and Byways in Galloway and Carrick* (London: MacMillan & Co., 1916), 156.

3. Herbert Maxwell, *The Place Names of Galloway* (1930; repr., Dalbeattie: Castlepoint Press, 2001), 151.

She Walks These Hills

1. Neil Wilson and Alan Murphy, *Scotland* (London: Lonely Planet Publications, 2004), 170.

Auld Kirk, New Kirk

1. Psalm 29:2.

2. Matthew 19:21.

Wild and Woolly

1. Charles Hill Dick, *Highways and Byways in Galloway and Carrick* (London: MacMillan & Co., 1916), 470.

2. David Williams, *Scotland's Best-Loved Driving Tours* (New York: Simon & Schuster Macmillan Co., 1998), 26.

An Afternoon of Villages

1. Charles Hill Dick, *Highways and Byways in Galloway and Carrick* (London: MacMillan & Co., 1916), 438.

2. Herbert Maxwell, *The Place Names of Galloway* (1930; repr., Dalbeattie: Castlepoint Press, 2001), 103.

3. Dick, *Highways and Byways,* 455.
4. Hugh Palmer, *The Most Beautiful Villages of Scotland* (London: Thames & Hudson, 2004), 49.

Banks o' the Nith

1. James Robertson, *The Public Roads and Bridges in Dumfriesshire 1650–1820* (Wigtown: G. C. Book Publishers, 1993), 189.
2. Mairi Robinson, ed., *Concise Scots Dictionary* (Edinburgh: Polygon, 1985), 635–37.
3. Charles Hill Dick, *Highways and Byways in Galloway and Carrick* (London: MacMillan & Co., 1916), 516.

Haste Ye Back

1. Charles Hill Dick, *Highways and Byways in Galloway and Carrick* (London: MacMillan & Co., 1916), 516.

A Wee Word

1. Dorothy L. Sayers, *Five Red Herrings* (1931; repr., London: Hodder & Stoughton, 1984), 5.

GLOSSARY

aboot—about

aften—often

ain—own

argle-bargle—contention, dispute

auchen—field

auld—old

banger—sausage

beadle—sexton

beadsman—almsman, pauper

belties—Galloway belted cattle

ben—mountain

bethankit—God be thanked

biggin—building

blissin—blessing

bogle—ghost, specter

boot—trunk of an automobile

brae—hill, slope

breakdown service—handles disabled automobiles

bridie—pie with meat filling

brig—bridge

brownie—benevolent sprite

byre—cowshed

cairn—heap of stones

canna—cannot

car park—parking lot

carse—low-lying land by a river

cauld—cold

chockablock—extremely full, crowded

clachan—hamlet, village

close—passageway, courtyard

coo—cow

cranachan—dessert made with cream and toasted oatmeal; also called cream crowdie

crannog—ancient lake dwelling

creepie—low chair, footstool

cruik—pothook

da—affectionate term for father

didna—did not

dinna—do not

doocot—dovecote

dreich—bleak, dismal

dry stane dyke—stone fence without mortar

dual carriageway—road with a median

eejit—dunderhead

elevensies—morning coffee break

en suite—attaching bed and bath

estate car—station wagon

fash—worry, trouble, vex

ferlie—superb, wonderful

flat—apartment

frae—from

fremmit—strange, unfamiliar, foreign

gaberlunzie—beggar, tramp

gaed—went

gallows—device for suspending a pot over a fire

girth—place of sanctuary

glebe—cultivated land owned by a parish

haar—cold mist or fog

hae—have

haggis—traditional Scottish dish of sheep offal and oatmeal, boiled in the sheep's stomach

harl—to roughcast with lime and small stones

haugh—level ground on the banks of a river

holidaymakers—vacationers

hoover—to vacuum

howff—favorite haunt, especially a public house

howlet—owl

i'—in

incomer—immigrant

ironmonger's—hardware store

jumper—woman's pullover sweater

keel—means of marking sheep for identification

kelpie—water demon

ken—to know, recognize

kirk—church

lade—channel bringing water to a mill

laird—landlord of an estate

lang—long

lie-in—sleeping later than usual

ling—variety of heather

linn—waterfall

loo—bathroom

lorry—truck

lug—hidden recess from which one might overhear the conversation in a room

ma—my

march—boundary line of a property

meikle—great, much

mem—madam

mercat—market

mony—many

mote—mound, embankment

och!—oh!

ochon—alas! oh sorrow!

oo aye!—yes! (from the French *oui*)

owre—over

panel beating—automobile body repair

peckish—somewhat hungry

pow—slow-moving, ditch-like stream

pram—perambulator, or baby carriage

prawn—shrimp

quid—one British pound sterling

quod—quoth, wrote

sae—so

sark—shirt

scrievin—gliding along easily

siller—silver

simmer—summer

sledge—sled

smirr—fine, misty rain

snuggery—comfortable, cozy room

sporran—men's purse or pouch, worn with a kilt

starters—appetizers

steik—fix, make immobile

syne—since, ago

telly—television

thrifite—money box

tickler—challenge, puzzle

toastie—sandwich on toasted bread

tolbooth—town prison

trews—close-fitting trousers

tup—ram

tuppence—twopence

twa—two

ugsome—gruesome, horrible

usefu'—useful

vennel—alley

wa'—wall

walcome—welcome

weel—well

wether—castrated male lamb

wha—who

wham—whom

whin—gorse, a prickly shrub

whinstone—dark-colored, fine-grained rocks

wholemeal—whole-wheat

wi'—with

wonky—shaky, unreliable

yett—gate

An Epic Journey through
⟶ Galloway of Old ⟵

*"Liz Curtis Higgs maps the human heart with indelible ink.
An extraordinary trilogy."*

—TERESA MEDEIROS,
New York Times best-selling author

A Dramatic Story All Her Own

*"An absorbing, well-crafted novel with a
gut-wrenching plot that will move readers.
Highly recommended."*

—*Library Journal* STARRED REVIEW

Available in bookstores and from online retailers.

WATERBROOK PRESS
www.waterbrookpress.com